TREKKING AUSTRIA'S ADLERWEG

THE EAGLE'S WAY
ACROSS THE AUSTRIAN ALPS IN TYROL

By Mike Wells

JUNIPER HOUSE, MURLEY MOSS,
OXENHOLME ROAD, KENDAL, CUMBRIA LA9 7RL
www.cicerone.co.uk

© Mike Wells 2023
Second edition 2023
ISBN: 978 1 78631 090 3
First edition 2012
ISBN: 978 1 85284 641 1

Printed in Singapore by KHL Printing using responsibly sourced paper.
A catalogue record for this book is available from the British Library.
All photographs are by the author unless otherwise stated.

Route mapping by Lovell Johns www.lovelljohns.com
Contains OpenStreetMap.org data © OpenStreetMap
contributors, CC-BY-SA. NASA relief data courtesy of ESRI

To Christine, who accompanied me through the Tyrol, until stopped by a broken leg, and Nassereith Bergrettungsdienst, who rescued her from Haimbachtal.

Updates to this Guide

While every effort is made by our authors to ensure the accuracy of guidebooks as they go to print, changes can occur during the lifetime of an edition. Any updates that we know of for this guide will be on the Cicerone website (www.cicerone.co.uk/1090/updates), so please check before planning your trip. We also advise that you check information about such things as transport, accommodation and shops locally. Even rights of way can be altered over time.

The route maps in this guide are derived from publicly available data, databases and crowd-sourced data. As such they have not been through the detailed checking procedures that would generally be applied to a published map from an official mapping agency, although we have reviewed them closely in the light of local knowledge as part of the preparation of this guide. We are always grateful for information about any discrepancies between a guidebook and the facts on the ground, sent by email to updates@cicerone.co.uk or by post to Cicerone, Juniper House, Murley Moss, Oxenholme Road, Kendal, LA9 7RL.

Register your book: To sign up to receive free updates, special offers and GPX files where available, create a Cicerone account and register your purchase via the 'My Account' tab at www.cicerone.co.uk.

Front cover: Adlerweg passes below Spritzkarspitze between Eng and Hohljoch, (photo: Tirol Werbung; photographer – Dominik Gigler) (Stage 9)

CONTENTS

Mountain safety

Every mountain walk has its dangers, and those described in this guidebook are no exception. All who walk or climb in the mountains should recognise this and take responsibility for themselves and their companions along the way. The author and publisher have made every effort to ensure that the information contained in this guide was correct when it went to press, but, except for any liability that cannot be excluded by law, they cannot accept responsibility for any loss, injury or inconvenience sustained by any person using this book.

International distress signal *(emergency only)*
Six blasts on a whistle (and flashes with a torch after dark) spaced evenly for one minute, followed by a minute's pause. Repeat until an answer is received. The response is three signals per minute followed by a minute's pause.

Helicopter rescue
The following signals are used to communicate with a helicopter:

Help needed:
raise both arms
above head to
form a 'Y'

Help not needed:
raise one arm
above head, extend
other arm downward

Emergency telephone numbers
Austria: Bergrettungsdienst (mountain rescue)
Tel 112 (emergency services number)

Weather forecasts
Austria: Bergwetter Österreich www.wetter.orf.at/tirol/bergwetter

Mountain rescue can be very expensive – be adequately insured.

ROUTE SUMMARY TABLE

Stage	Start	Finish	Via	Distance (km)	Ascent (m)	Descent (m)	Page
Kaisergebirge							
1	St Johann in Tirol	Gaudeamushütte		13	1100	510	48
2	Gaudeamushütte	Schiesti (Hintersteinersee)		14.5	800	1140	55
3	Schiesti (Hintersteinersee)	Kufstein		11	820	510	60
Brandenberger Alpen and Rofangebirge							
4	Langkampfen	Buchackeralm		11	1370	540	66
5	Buchackeralm	Pinegg		16.5	920	1570	72
6	Pinegg	Steinberg am Rofan		18	1170	850	77
7	Steinberg am Rofan	Mauritzalm		18	1590	760	82
Karwendelgebirge							
8	Maurach	Lamsenjochhütte		17	1030	60	92
9	Lamsenjochhütte	Falkenhütte		12.5	820	930	99
10	Falkenhütte	Karwendelhaus		9	460	540	104
11	Karwendelhaus	Hallerangeralm	Birkkarspitze	14	1440	1440	108
11A	Karwendelhaus	Hallerangeralm	Karwendeltal	32.5	850	850	113
12	Hallerangeralm	Hafelekarhaus		13	1150	650	118

Innsbruck and Patscherkofel

12A	Innsbruck city tour		2.5			124
13	Patscherkofel	Tulfeinalm	8	300	230	130

Wettersteingebirge and Mieminger Gebirge

14	Hochzirl	Solsteinhaus	7	940	60	137
15	Solsteinhaus	Leutasch (Weidach)	18	800	1490	140
16	Leutasch (Weidach)	Ehrwald	24	600	720	145
17	Ehrwald	Loreahütte	19	1170	1189	153

Lechtaler Alpen

18	Loreahütte	Anhalter Hütte	16	1260	1240	161
19	Anhalter Hütte	Hanauer Hütte	12.5	750	870	166
20	Hanauer Hütte	Württemberger Haus	11	1300	1000	171
21	Württemberger Haus	Memminger Hütte	7	670	650	175
22	Memminger Hütte	Ansbacher Hütte	10	1040	910	178
23	Ansbacher Hütte	Leutkircher Hütte	12.5	970	1080	181
24	Leutkircher Hütte	Arlbergpass	13.5	630	1100	185

Lechtal valley

19A	Boden	Häselgehr	15.5	330	680	191
20A	Häselgehr	Steeg	19.5	220	100	195
21A	Steeg	St Anton am Arlberg	19.5	1190	1030	201

Klamml gorge on the way to Gruttenhütte (photo: Tirol Werbung; photographer – Jens Schwarz) (Stage 2)

INTRODUCTION

Eagle motif found at key points along the Adlerweg

There are two ways to soar among the magnificent peaks of the Tyrolean Alps: one is in an aeroplane as you fly into Innsbruck; the other, more challenging and exciting, is to follow the Adlerweg as it crosses the entire length of the Tyrol from St Johann in Tirol in the east to St Anton am Arlberg in the west. Not only will you experience the Wilder Kaiser, Brandenberg, Rofan, Karwendel and Lechtaler Alps close up, but you should also have spectacular distant views of Austria's other principal mountain ranges, including the peaks of Grossglockner and Grossvenediger and the Tuxer and Stubai Alps. As a bonus, you will pass immediately below the towering south face of Zugspitze, Bavaria's (and Germany's) highest mountain.

The main route of the Adlerweg is a 326km long-distance path traversing the Austrian Tyrol, keeping mostly to the mountains that form the northern side of Inntal, the Inn valley. It is made up of 24 stages, with a total height gain of just over 23,000m. The route is primarily for experienced mountain walkers, but this guide includes a number of easier variant stages that circumvent the airier parts, thus making the Adlerweg doable for all types of walker. Well maintained and waymarked throughout, the Adlerweg follows established mountain and valley tracks. While it is not

a 'peak-bagging' path, it does offer the opportunity to visit the tops of a few mountains, including Rofanspitze (2259m) (Stage 7) and Birkkarspitze (2749m) (Stage 11). The full route takes a fit walker about three weeks to complete; however, if you wish to take things more gently, it is possible to undertake the Adlerweg as two 2-week walks, breaking the journey in Innsbruck. Most of the stages are well connected by public transport (train, postbus, cable car or chairlift), making it possible to tackle shorter trips as day excursions or weekend overnight breaks.

The path was conceived and implemented by Tirol Werbung, the regional tourist promotion agency, who named it the Eagle's Way (*Adler* being German for 'eagle'); when overlaid on the map, its silhouette appears in the shape of an eagle, the outspread wings of which reach from one end of the Tyrol to the other, with Innsbruck, in the middle, as its head. The proud eagle is said to represent the feelings of freedom and independence, power and wisdom, grandeur and dignity, which you can experience when hiking the Eagle's Way. In addition to the main route, there is a separate shorter (but higher!) kleiner Adlerweg (Eaglet path) of nine stages in Ost Tirol, which is not covered by this book.

Since the first edition of this guide was published ten years ago, Tirol Werbung has made a number of significant changes to the route, particularly in Brandenberg and in the Lechtaler Alpen/Lechtal valley.

Overall, this has made the route a more challenging walk, one for experienced mountain walkers. This guide includes all of Tirol Werbung's changes. In addition, some routes from the previous edition have been retained where they provide easier alternatives. Although no longer way-marked as part of the Adlerweg, they are all well maintained and very walkable routes. Taken overall, the routes in this book should prove attractive to all grades of walker, not just those with prior mountain-walking experience.

Hiking in the Tyrol would not be complete without Austria's legendary hospitality and local cuisine. Since overnight accommodation in the form of serviced mountain *Hütten* (refuges), inns, guesthouses or hotels can be found at the end of each day's walk, all you will need to carry is a sheet sleeping bag. Everywhere along the way there are convenient places to eat and drink. These range from simple alpine pasture huts in the mountains, offering locally produced fare, to award-winning restaurants in the towns and valleys. On most stages, frequent water fountains and springs provide a safe source of drinking water.

A wide variety of animals and plants can be found. The lower meadows are carpeted with wildflowers in late spring, while once the snow disappears the upper slopes come alive with alpine plants, including edelweiss and gentian. Chamois, ibex and marmots can be seen throughout the route. However, as you are walking the Eagle's Way, the creature you will most likely want to find is the eponymous golden eagle. Keep a good lookout and you may see one soaring around the highest peaks. If, however, wild eagles prove illusive, the route passes Innsbruck Alpen zoo, where there are two captive golden eagles.

The Tyrol tourist organisation describes the Adlerweg as 'arguably the most beautiful long-distance trail in Austria'. Does it live up to this claim? That is for you to decide. Walk it and see!

Note Throughout this guide the English spelling of Tyrol is used, except for proper nouns such as 'Count of Tirol', 'St Johann in Tirol' or 'Tirol Werbung', where the German 'Tirol' is used.

BACKGROUND

Austria

Located in the centre of the continent, and straddling the Alps, Austria is one of Europe's smaller countries in terms of size and population (9 million inhabitants). It shares borders with Germany (with which it has a common language), Czechia, Slovakia, Hungary, Slovenia, Italy, Switzerland and Liechtenstein. Its position in relation to the Danube, one of Europe's most important waterways, to the north, and the Brenner, the most accessible alpine pass, to the south, has made Austria the crossroads of central Europe.

During the 18th and 19th centuries, Austria's political, economic and military significance surpassed its modest size. After the turning back of Islamic incursions into Europe at the Battle of Vienna (1683), a long period of rule by one family enabled Austria to maintain strong stable government and build a pan-European empire. The Hapsburg emperors ruled until defeat in World War 1 led to the break-up of the Austro-Hungarian Empire by the Treaty of St Germain in 1919.

A period of economic and political uncertainty during the 1920s and 1930s (when many mountain refuges fell into disrepair) was followed by the *Anschluss* political union with Germany in 1938 and Austrian participation on the axis side in World War 2. After the conflict, government was briefly divided between the victorious allied powers until the current republic was established in 1955. Austria joined the EU in 1995, and the subsequent signing of the Schengen Agreement led to the removal of border controls.

Austria is a federal republic of nine states. The majority of the population lives in four lowland states, which include the capital Vienna, to the north and east of the country. Population density in the alpine states of the south and west, including Tyrol, is much lower.

Tyrol

Tyrol sits south-west of the bulk of Austria, between the states of Salzburg (east) and Vorarlberg (west). Its dominant feature is the

Descending from Memminger Hütte into Parseiertal, with Parseierspitze in the distance (photo: Tirol Werbung; photographer – Dominik Gigler) (Stage 22)

deep west–east gash of the Inn valley, between the northern limestone Alps (Nördlichen Kalkalpen) and the central high Alps, with most of the 760,000 population living along this axis. Tyrol's northern border, with Germany, runs through the North Kalkalpen, and its southern, Italian, border crosses the central Alps.

Tyrol's emergence as an identifiable state began in the 11th century when the Counts of Tirol from Meran (today Merano in northern Italy) gradually extended their control over the whole region. When the last count (or rather countess) died heirless, control passed to the Austrian Hapsburgs, with Tyrol becoming part of Austria in 1363. Apart from a brief period of Bavarian rule during the Napoleonic wars, it has remained Austrian ever since. However, Tyrol today is much smaller than Hapsburg Tyrol, as the peace treaties that concluded World War 1 transferred sovereignty over Sud Tirol and Trient to Italy.

Apart from Reutte in the northwest and Kitzbühel in the east, the main towns are spread along the Inn valley, from Kufstein and Schwaz in the lower valley to Imst and Landeck in the upper valley. By far the largest population centre, the state capital Innsbruck is located in the middle valley.

Tyrol is a region of open countryside. Only 12% of the state can be used for human habitation, with 35% forest, 30% pasture and 22% barren mountains. As a result, the Tyrolean economy has been based on agriculture (mostly dairy farming), timber and mining (silver, lead, zinc, salt, limestone, silica sand and shale oil). Secondary industries have grown up using these raw materials, including wooden building materials, glass, cement and chemicals. Other light industry, originally based upon the ready availability of power from mountain streams but now using hydroelectric power, includes iron smelting, agricultural tools and machinery, railway carriages and electric power generators. In the 20th century, year-round tourism (winter sports and summer touring) became a major part of the state economy, while one of the largest employers in Innsbruck is its university.

THE ADLERWEG

The Adlerweg is a project promoted by Tirol Werbung (the state tourism promotional agency) to encourage walkers to explore more of the region. It came to fruition in 2005 with the opening of the main route between St Johann in Tirol, in the east of Tyrol, and St Anton am Arlberg, on the western border with Vorarlberg. The route had no 'new' paths, being a series of existing paths and tracks linked by common signposting, usually by means of adding an Adlerweg motif to existing signposts.

There was, however, a political dimension to the project. Tirol Werbung is funded by regional government and by payments from all of the local government areas (*Gemeinden*) in the region. As a result, there was pressure to ensure the route visited as many Gemeinden as possible. In consequence, the route was extended by the addition of 88 regional paths that formed a series of legs running off the original route, thus taking the Adlerweg name into many other parts of Tyrol. Unsurprisingly, a degree of confusion crept in. Mapmakers were encouraged to add 'Adlerweg' or the eagle motif to their maps of the region. This was done without discriminating between the main route, easier variants or regional extensions, with 'Adlerweg' soon popping up all over the map, making it difficult to identify the correct route.

A change of policy in 2015 abandoned this proliferation, with the Adlerweg now confined to one continuous route of 24 stages between St Johann in Tirol and St Anton am Arlberg, plus nine stages forming a separate 'Eaglet' path in Ost Tirol. The stages that now form the main route have varying degrees of difficulty, although none requires climbing skills or equipment. They average 13.5km in length with 950m of ascent. The easier alternatives described in this guide are no longer officially part of the Adlerweg. However, as most were part of the previous network, they are well-maintained paths which are still labelled as the Adlerweg on some older maps.

One aspect of the Adlerweg that makes it different from most other long-distance paths is the use of various modes of public transport to speed access to and descent from the mountains. As a result, you will encounter cable cars, chairlifts, trains, buses, a funicular and a tram all integrated into the route. It is possible to avoid some of the cable cars and chairlifts, and this guide indicates where such options occur.

THE NATURAL ENVIRONMENT

Physical geography

The Alps, which form a high mountain barrier between northern and southern Europe, are some of the youngest European mountains. They were formed approximately 50 million years ago when the African and European tectonic plates collided, pushing the land up. The Alps run west to east through Austria and consist of three parallel mountain ranges: the high, mainly granite, central Alps flanked by the slightly lower northern and southern calcareous limestone chains. The Adlerweg traverses the most northerly of these, the Nördlichen Kalkalpen, following the range from east to west. For much of its length there are extensive views south across the deep glacial defile of the Inn valley, with the higher permanently snow-capped central Alps on the horizon and occasional views north across the Alpine foothills to Bavaria.

Krahnsattel, with the view north across Gruba bowl to Rosskopf (Stage 7A)

The chain is broken into a series of blocks by a number of north–south glacial river valleys that have broken through the mountains. As their name implies, the Calcareous Alps are composed mostly of porous limestone, with the exact composition of this limestone varying from block to block. The two most significant geological aspects of the region are glaciation and karst country.

During the great ice ages, ice sheets covered all of central and northern Europe. As the ice retreated, great glaciers carved deep valleys through the Austrian Alps, the deepest and longest forming the Inn valley. Running east from the Engadin region of Switzerland right across Tyrol, where it separates the northern and central Alpine ranges, it reaches the Danube basin beyond Kufstein. Along its length, the Inn is joined by lateral glacial valleys flowing in from the north and south. Most of the glaciers have long since melted and only a few remain, mostly in the high central Alps. There are none on the Adlerweg.

The enduring legacies left behind by the retreating glaciers are characteristic deep U-shaped valleys and morainic lakes. Throughout the walk you will be able to trace old glacial flows, from smooth bowl-shaped cirques surrounded on three sides by high jagged mountains, down stepped valleys blocked by terminal moraines containing either morainic lakes or the dried-up beds of earlier lakes. The descent from Birkkarspitze (Stage 11) is almost a geography lesson, with every kind of glacial feature on show.

15

Glacial cirque below Birkkarspitze (Stage 11)

The receding glaciers stripped much of the topsoil, leaving large areas of smooth limestone exposed. The steady slow erosion of this bare limestone by acidic rainwater causes limestone pavements to form. While karst pavements are seen on the surface (notably above Zireineralm, Stage 7), most karst features are hidden below ground in a series of sinkholes and cave systems. Zireinersee lake (Stage 7) is a karst lake with no visible outlet, while the Hundsalm Eishöhle cave (Stage 4) is part of a karst cave system.

Walking the Adlerweg, you will encounter a few morainic lakes, some trapped by terminal moraines and some by lateral. The most notable is Achensee, the unique geography of which is described in Stage 8, while the descent from Fern pass (Stage 17) provides excellent views of a series of turquoise-coloured lakes, each trapped by its own moraine. Lateral lakes line the Inn valley between Kramsach and Wörgl. There are many dried-up lake beds, the most obvious being the Moos, between Ehrwald and Lermoos (Stage 17), and in the Hinterautal valley (Stage 11). Extensive beaches of glacial fluor (white limestone sand eroded by the glaciers) often indicate the location of an ancient lake. This same fluor, brought down from the glaciers of the Engadin, colours the river Inn white.

This is an ever-changing landscape. Frequent landsides and washouts either block or widen rivers. Attempts are made each year to restore paths after winter damage, but

when deterioration becomes irrepara-
ble, paths may be closed or diverted.

Plants

The overwhelming determinant of
plant life found along the Adlerweg
is altitude, particularly the treeline.
This, the altitude beyond which
trees cannot survive, is found around
1800m on north-facing slopes but
can reach nearly 2000m at favoured
south-facing locations. At lower altitudes, up to approximately 1400m,
mixed forests dominate, with broadleaf deciduous trees like beech and
oak growing alongside conifers.
Woodland flowers and berries, particularly wild raspberries, grow in
clearings between the trees. A wide
range of edible fungi is in evidence,
and local residents can often be
found collecting them for the kitchen.

Alpenrose

As altitude increases, so mixed
forest gives way to coniferous forest with spruce, pine, fir, juniper
and larch all in evidence. Of note is
Zirbe, a pine with candelabra-shaped
branches, the smooth wood of which
is favoured for woodcarving and ver-
nacular furniture. Zirbe grows close to
the treeline, particularly on the upper
north slopes of Patscherkofel, where it
gives its name to the Zirbenweg (Stage
13). Just below the treeline, full-grown
trees give way to *Krummholz* (dwarf
conifers), which grow sideways rather
than upwards.

The high meadow above the
treeline is the alpine zone, rich with
alpine flowers. Of particular note,
and easy to spot, are blue harebells
(*campanula*). Slightly rarer are vivid
blue trumpet gentians and the pink-
flowered evergreen shrub, alpenrose.
Most renowned, but rarest of all, is
the white edelweiss. Above this zone,
where lingering snow often covers
sparse grass on thin soil and bare
rock, you can find bright-pink flower
cushions of rock jasmine and various
lichen and mosses.

Wildlife

A wide variety of birds, mammals,
reptiles and insects are found along
the Adlerweg. Many of these, including foxes, red squirrels, hares and
roe deer, can be found in Britain,
but there are three mammals in particular that epitomise the high alpine
environment.

Ibex (steinbock)

The grassy higher slopes with rocky outcrops are marmot country. These large rodents are instantly recognisable by the piercing 'wolf-whistle' warning calls of the adult males. Living as family groups in burrows 3m deep, they eat plant greenery, growing to a maximum weight of 6kg by late September. They hibernate beneath the snows, living off their body fat, until they re-emerge much slimmed down in April. Marmots are found at many places along the route, and sightings are guaranteed.

The second most likely high-mountain mammal to be seen is the *Gams* (chamois). These timid, skittish creatures of the antelope family inhabit barely accessible high slopes where they move with amazing sure-footedness. They are often heard before they are seen, as they run across the slopes generating a rocky clatter from falling scree. Fully grown, they reach just 75cm in height and have short straightish horns that hook backwards towards the tip. They live in groups of up to 30 individuals, mostly females and juveniles, with older males living a solitary life.

The *Steinbock* (ibex), a herbivorous member of the goat family, is the largest of the three mountain mammals. Males grow to 1m with large backward-facing horns, while females are about half this size. Days are spent on rocky slopes above the treeline, where they are safe from predators. In late afternoon, they descend to feed on leaves and shrubs in the forest, where they can sometimes be seen standing on their hind legs to reach juicy higher leaves. Ibex were severely depleted by hunting, but numbers are now increasing.

Black alpine choughs (*Alpendohle*) with yellow beaks and red legs are ubiquitous birds, performing aerial acrobatics over the mountaintops. Pairing for life, they nest on rocky cliff ledges at a higher altitude than any other bird species. Seemingly unafraid of humans, they will often try to plunder your lunchtime sandwiches.

The only way to be sure to see a golden eagle (*Adler*) is to visit Innsbruck Alpen zoo (Stage 12), where a rather sad-looking captive pair inhabit a large aviary. There are 12 pairs living in Karwendelgebirge, although if you are lucky enough to see one in the wild it is unlikely to be more than a mere dot high in the sky. They are ferocious predators with a wingspan of 2m and powerful talons that can seize creatures as large as small roe deer.

National parks and protected areas
Although the route doesn't take in any designated national parks, much of it passes through areas with a high level of environmental protection or national forest. The Wilder Kaiser, Karwendel, Arnspitze and most of the Lechtal valley are *Naturschutzgebieten* (NSG, nature protected areas), while other places are *Landschaftsschutzgebieten* (LSG, similar to Sites of Special Scientific Interest in the UK). Brandenberg and Tegestal are national forests managed by Österreichische Bundesforste (ÖBF). Proposals have been made to create national parks, but this high level of protection has been blocked by opposition from hunting interests, which are strong in Tyrol. Camping, lighting fires, disturbing wildlife or removing plants are prohibited in these areas.

Golden eagle in Innsbruck Alpen zoo (Stage 12A)

PREPARATION

When to go
The Adlerweg is a summer walk, with a season from mid June to early October, although after heavy winter snowfall significant snow may remain at higher altitudes until mid July, with

HOLIDAYS IN AUSTRIA

There are a number of Austrian national holidays during the summer. On these days banks are closed and public transport operates *Feiertage* (holiday) timetables, which are usually the same as Sunday schedules.

* Easter: variable, late March to late April
* May day: 1 May
* Ascension Day: variable, May
* Whit Monday: variable, mid May to mid June
* Corpus Christi: variable, late May to late June
* Assumption Day: 15 August
* National Day: 26 October
* All Saints' Day: 1 November

School summer holidays run from mid July to mid September. Most towns and villages have summer festival days, and from mid September to early October many villages celebrate *Almabetriebsfest*, when cows are welcomed back from summer mountain pastures. In Innsbruck, the Battle of Bergisel is commemorated on 14 August.

early season falls commencing in early September. In a few locations, snow can remain all year. Opening and closing dates of mountain refuges and restaurants reflect the walkability of the paths, with refuges on the highest stages not opening until late June/early July and closing from mid September. The most popular period for walking in Tyrol is mid July–late August, and this is when you may encounter busy refuges, particularly those such as Karwendel Haus (Stage 10), which also takes in the Vital Route mountain-bike trail and the Munich–Venice long-distance footpath, or Memminger Hütte (Stage 21), which is also on transalpine path E5. You will meet very few walkers actually

following the Adlerweg, although you will encounter many day walkers. Parts of the walk can be attempted in winter, but as this requires specialist skills and equipment it is not covered in this guide.

Apart from late-lying snow, or early snowfalls, the going underfoot is usually excellent. The underlying stratum is limestone, resulting in good drainage with very few places prone to boggy conditions. After rain, or in mist, rocks can get very slippery and some of the stages over exposed rock can become treacherous. These parts of the trail are usually protected by fixed steel cables, providing security in slippery conditions.

How long will it take?

The Adlerweg is not a walk to take lightly. It is possible to walk the entire route in 16 days, but this requires an average of 8hr walking every day, covering over 19km and ascending 1375m, mostly above 1000m and sometimes above 2000m. To achieve this daily distance and ascent at altitude you need a high level of fitness.

21-day schedule					
Day	Start	Finish	Distance (km)	Time (h:m)	Ascent (m)
1	St Johann in Tirol	Gruttenhütte	14.5	06:30	1470
2	Gruttenhütte	Steinbergalm	19.0	07:00	1060
3	Steinbergalm	Buchackeralm	16.0	07:10	1560
4	Buchackeralm	Pinegg	16.5	06:30	920
5	Pinegg	Steinberg am Rofan	18.0	05:30	1170
6	Steinberg am Rofan	Mauritzalm	18.0	07:00	1590
7	Mauritzalm	Lamsenjochhütte	17.0	05:00	1030
8	Lamsenjochhütte	Karwendelhaus	21.5	08:00	1280
9	Karwendelhaus	Hallerangeralm	14.0	08:00	1440
10	Hallerangeralm	Innsbruck	13.0	05:30	1150
11	Innsbruck	Solsteinhaus	15.0	05:30	1240
12	Solsteinhaus	Weidach	18.0	06:30	800
13	Weidach	Lermoos	27.5	07:15	630
14	Lermoos	Loreahütte	15.5	05:45	1140
15	Loreahütte	Anhalter Hütte	16.0	06:30	1260
16	Anhalter Hütte	Hanauer Hütte	12.5	04:15	750
17	Hanauer Hütte	Württemberger Haus	11.0	07:00	1300
18	Württemberger Haus	Memminger Hütte	7.0	05:00	670
19	Memminger Hütte	Ansbacher Hütte	10.0	06:00	1040
20	Ansbacher Hütte	Leutkircher Hütte	12.5	07:00	970
21	Leutkircher Hütte	Arlbergpass	13.5	05:00	630
		Total	**326**	**132:00**	**23100**
		Daily average	**15.5**	**06:15**	**1100**

If you wish to take it more gently, 6hr walking, covering 15km per day, will enable you to complete the walk in 3 weeks. Moreover, this will allow you time to see more of the region and visit a number of attractions passed en route, such as a cruise on Achensee, a visit to the Alpen zoo or a cable car to the summit of Zugspitze. An even more leisurely approach would be to walk the route in two fortnightly trips, breaking your journey at Innsbruck, which has an airport and international train connections.

Each of the 24 stages can be walked in a day, some in less than this, allowing 1½ or 2 stages to be combined. However, some stages, particularly Stage 11 (the crossing of Birkkarspitze from Karwendel Haus

16-day schedule					
Day	Start	Finish	Distance (km)	Time (h:m)	Ascent (m)
1	St Johann in Tirol	Bärnstatt	23.5	09:45	1780
2	Bärnstatt	Buchackeralm	26.0	10:55	2300
3	Buchackeralm	Pinegg	16.5	06:30	920
4*	Pinegg	Mauritzalm	22.0	07:30	1660
5	Mauritzalm	Lamsenjochhütte	17.0	05:00	1030
6	Lamsenjochhütte	Karwendelhaus	21.5	08:00	1280
7	Karwendelhaus	Hallerangeralm	14.0	08:00	1440
8	Hallerangeralm	Innsbruck	13.0	05:30	1150
9	Innsbruck	Solsteinhaus	15.0	05:30	1240
10	Solsteinhaus	Gaistalalm	28.5	08:15	1160
11	Gaistalalm	Fernstein	28.0	08:30	340
12	Fernstein	Anhalter Hütte	20.5	09:15	2330
13	Anhalter Hütte	Steinseehütte	17.0	07:30	1340
14	Steinseehütte	Memminger Hütte	13.5	08:45	1380
15	Memminger Hütte	Kaiserjochhaus	18.0	11:00	1700
16	Kaiserjochhaus	Arlbergpass	18.0	07:00	940
		Total	312	127:00	21990
		Daily average	19.5	08:00	1375

*Day 4 goes directly from Pinegg to Mauritzalm, avoiding Steinberg

Looking up Rotlechtal, with the cliffs of Heiterwand flanking the valley (Stage 18)

to Hallerangeralm) and most of the stages in the Lechtaler Alpen, take a full day.

Tourist offices

Tourist offices operate at both regional and local levels. Tirol Werbung in Innsbruck is responsible for marketing Tyrol as a tourist destination and part of this role involves setting up, managing and promoting the Adlerweg.

A popular pastime of Tyrolean walkers is to collect the passport-type stamps available at every refuge, at many hotels and guesthouses and at dedicated 'stamping stations'. Tirol Werbung has produced a *Stempelblatt* (stamping card) to collect these stamps. Alternatively, you can use the SummitLynx app which will work with your GPS to track progress along the Adlerweg (www.summitlynx.com). When you have completed your walk, you can claim an eagle pin with bronze, silver or gold wings, depending on how many stamps you have collected or how many stages you have completed on the app. A few pages at the end of this book have been left clear as another way to collect your stamps.

Every town and some villages have their own local tourist office, which can provide local maps and full details of accommodation and events in their area. Opening times vary and smaller offices may not be open at weekends. Staff are generally very helpful and speak good English. Advice is provided on all grades of accommodation and most offices will call to check vacancies and make reservations. They cannot make reservations 'out of area' but are usually willing to phone the relevant local office and relay your requirements. Contact details for all tourist offices can be found in Appendix B.

Alpine Club

Founded in 1862, the Österreichischer Alpenverein (ÖAV, Austrian Alpine Club) has over 600,000 members involved in all kinds of mountain activities. It is responsible for building, maintaining and modernising a large number of mountain refuges, waymarking and maintaining footpaths, producing maps and guidebooks and aiding the independent rescue service. It works closely with the Deutscher Alpenverein (DAV, German Alpine Club), which owns and operates the majority of mountain refuges on the Adlerweg. Many of these were built by DAV sections early in the 20th century to provide mountain recreational facilities for members throughout Germany. After World War 2 they were placed under Austrian control, but since the sixties have been returned to their former owners.

Facilities can be used by anyone, but members obtain specific benefits, including substantial discounts on accommodation, annual rescue and repatriation insurance plus maps and guidebooks at discounted prices. Benefits are available on a reciprocal basis with other national alpine clubs, including DAV.

If you are planning to walk the Adlerweg, and are not a member of an alpine club, you are strongly recommended to join ÖAV. If you are British, the easiest way to do this is to become a member of AAC (UK), also known as Sektion Britannia. AAC (UK) is a fully fledged section of ÖAV with over 12,000 members. Annual membership in 2023 cost £57, with a £44 reduced rate for seniors over 65 years, juniors under 27 years and members' partners. Contact details are in Appendix C.

GETTING THERE

By rail

You can travel from London to St Johann in a day by leaving in the early morning and arriving late evening. Departure is from St Pancras, using Eurostar to reach either Brussels or Paris.

- Eurostar to Brussels, then Brussels to Frankfurt and on to Munich using DB ICE trains. Munich to Wörgl by DB, with ÖBB connection at Wörgl for St Johann.
- Eurostar to Paris Nord, then a 10min walk to Paris Est for an ICE train to Stuttgart and on to Munich. Munich to Wörgl by DB, with ÖBB connection at Wörgl for St Johann.
- Return from St Anton to London can be done in one day by using an ÖBB Railjet train to Zurich

then Lyria train to Paris and Eurostar to London.

Tickets are available from Rail Europe or Trainline. Contact details are in Appendix C.

By air

Various airlines fly directly to Munich, Innsbruck or Salzburg.

- From Munich airport, frequent S-trains (S8 to Munich Ost, 37min, and S1 to Munich Hbf, 40min) link the airport with the DB German rail network. Regular DB trains connect Munich via Rosenheim and Kufstein to Wörgl in the Inn valley. ÖBB (Austrian railways) trains connect Wörgl with St Johann.
- From Salzburg airport, bus route 2 runs to Salzburg Hbf from where ÖBB trains enable you to reach St Johann via Bischofshofen.

- From Innsbruck airport there is a bus to Innsbruck Hbf for regular ÖBB trains to Wörgl and St Johann.
- Return from St Anton by ÖBB trains to Innsbruck then connect for Munich via Kufstein or Garmisch, or for Salzburg via Kufstein or via Bischofshofen. As an alternative return route from St Anton, take a Railjet train direct to Zurich. Frequent trains connect Zurich Hbf with Zurich airport, where various airlines fly to UK airports.

By road

From the UK you can use either a Eurotunnel shuttle train or a car ferry to reach Calais from where *autoroutes/Autobahnen* (motorways) can be followed across Belgium and Germany to Munich and Kufstein,

In high season a vintage bus runs between Pertisau and Gramaialm (Stage 8)

then local roads to St Johann via
Elmau. The total distance from Calais
to St Johann is 1100km, with a driv-
ing time of at least 12hr. Leaving your
car in St Johann, you can return by
train from St Anton via Innsbruck and
Wörgl to pick it up.

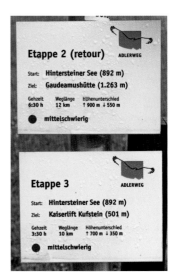

Signs at the start and finish of each stage

NAVIGATION

Path grading

Throughout the Tyrol a standard system is used to grade the level of experience, skills, fitness and equipment
required to walk the mountain paths.
There are three grades: *Wanderweg,
roter Bergweg* and *schwarzer
Bergweg*. The system is colour
coded, with white (Wanderweg), red
(roter Bergweg) or black (schwarzer
Bergweg) usually appearing in a small
circle on signposts. The grade relates
to the most difficult part of the stage.
Often when only part of a stage is
graded black, alternative easier routes
are available to avoid the difficult section. The official grade of the treks in
this guide is supplied in the introduc-
tion to each stage.

A Wanderweg (white) is an easily
accessible footpath that is generally
wide with only slight gradients. There
is no exposure, and neither a head
for heights nor mountain equipment
is needed. Only one stage (Stage 16
from Leutasch to Ehrwald) is classified
as a Wanderweg, although it makes
up for its easy-going classification by
being the longest stage of all.

Roter Bergweg (red) trails have
a moderate level of difficulty and
are sometimes steep or narrow, with
short cable-aided sections possible.
Surefootedness, a reasonable head
for heights and appropriate physical
condition are required. No specialist mountain equipment is needed,
although a good pair of walking boots
and appropriate clothing is essential.
There are 13 roter Bergweg stages plus
one other, which although graded red
has a black section; there is, however,
an alternative route to bypass the difficult part.

Schwarzer Bergweg (black) trails
are steeper, more difficult stages;
they are often narrow with aided
scrambling sections and exposure to

steep drops. Experience of mountain walking is essential, together with a reasonable level of physical fitness, surefootedness and a good head for heights. However, these stages are walks or scrambles – not climbs – so no specialist mountaineering equipment is needed. The Adlerweg has nine schwarzer Bergweg stages. There are, however, alternative routes to bypass all these black stages.

Waymarking

The Adlerweg network is marked with a standard series of signs and signposts. At the beginning of most stages a signboard shows the whole stage, including timing, distance and height difference. En route signposting using yellow fingerposts is almost universal and excellent. These fingerposts can be found at most path junctions, and even in remote locations they leave little doubt as to which path to take. They usually show the next few destinations as well as estimated walking times and path grade (white/red/black). The Adlerweg is identified on these signs by an eagle silhouette motif, and sometimes by name.

Between fingerposts, the path is identified by the use of red and white paint flashes on convenient surfaces, such as rocks, trees, walls and buildings. These provide waymarking over difficult ground and are essential through forests, across scree and in open pasture where the path may sometimes be indistinct. Occasionally, small cairns mark the route, but in misty conditions paint flashes are considerably more visible. On some stages, where the Adlerweg uses another established path, such

Red and white painted waymarks are used to show the way

Gramaialm at the head of Falzthurnalm, with Lamsenspitze behind (Stage 8)

as Wilder Kaiser Steig in Stage 2, other coloured paint flashes may be encountered.

Guidebooks

Tirol Werbung produces an overall free map and *Tourenbuch* (guide) to the route in English, which can be obtained through their official Adlerweg website (www.tirol.at/reisefuehrer/sport/wandern/adlerweg). The website also has downloadable descriptions, maps and GPS tracks for every stage, accommodation and refreshment lists and general information about the Adlerweg.

- There are two guidebooks in German. Conrad Stein publishes *Wanderführer Österreich: Adlerweg* by Christian Rupp (2015) ISBN 9783866864696,

while Rother publishes *Adlerweg: Vom Wilden Kaiser zum Arlberg* by Anne Haertel in their Wanderführer series (second edition 2021) ISBN 9783763344901.

- The Alpenverein Hütte Book contains details of all alpine refuges in Austria, Germany and Sud Tirol. It is in German with an English key explaining symbols and is available from the Austrian Alpine Club UK.

Maps

The maps in this guide are sourced from commercially available mapping and reproduced at a scale of 1:50,000. While they are accurate, they are not as detailed as maps produced by specialist map publishers, particularly those at 1:25,000. Maps

RECOMMENDED MAPS TO COVER THE ENTIRE ADLERWEG ROUTE

- ÖAV 1:25,000 8, 6, 5/3, 5/2, 5/1, 4/3, 4/2, 4/1, 3/4, 3/3, 3/2
- Kompass 1:35,000 036 (covering Zirbenweg)
- Freytag & Berndt 1:50,000 321 (covering Brandenberg)

from three publishers cover the route using varying scales. Sheet numbers for the relevant maps are shown in the introductory box of each stage.

Österreichischer Alpenverein (ÖAV) maps cover almost 90% of the route at 1:25,000. There is neither coverage of the walk-in from St Johann to Rummlerhof nor of Brandenberger Stages 4, 5 and part of Stage 6, with Stage 13 covered only at 1:50,000. These maps give the most comprehensive coverage of the Adlerweg, but 13 sheets are required (11 ÖAV plus two from other publishers). Contours are at 20m intervals overlaid with a black hairline depiction of rock features. Sheets required: 8, 6, 5/3, 5/2, 5/1, 4/3, 4/2, 4/1, 3/4, 3/3, 3/2 (all 1:25,000) and 31/5 (1:50,000). If you are going to use the alternative Lechtal valley route to avoid the Lechtaler Alpen, you will need map 2/2 instead of map 3/3.

A USB memory stick containing all ÖAV maps is available. You can download this to your GPS navigational device, or you can create your own strip maps of the route, at a scale of your choice, which provides considerable weight- and space-saving advantages compared with carrying printed maps.

Freytag & Berndt (FB) cover the route in six sheets at 1:50,000. In addition, there is a 1:35,000 map of the Lechtaler Alpen around St Anton, which can be used to access greater detail on the last four stages. Maps come with an enclosed booklet (in German) that provides tourist information, paths and walking routes, mountain refuges and guesthouses, and GPS details of key points shown on the maps. Contours are at 100m intervals. Sheets required: 301, 321, 322, 241, 352 and 351. Sheet 5504 (1:25,000) can be used to supplement 351.

Kompass (K) covers the route, with two maps at 1:25,000, two at 1:35,000 and three at 1:50,000. The maps come with a booklet giving details of towns, villages, mountain paths and accommodation. Contours are at 40m intervals. Details and path markings are clearer than on Freytag & Berndt maps. The larger scale maps are simply enlargements of the 1:50,000, making them easier to read but with no greater detail. Sheets required: 09 and 026 (1:25,000), 027 and 036 (1:35,000), plus 5, 8 and 24 (1:50,000).

All commercial maps are available from leading map shops,

including Stanfords in London and The Map Shop in Upton upon Severn, and are widely available in Austria. ÖAV maps and a USB memory stick can also be obtained from either ÖAV in Innsbruck or the ÖAV Britannia Section (www.alpenverein.at/britannia) at a discounted price for members.

GPS

GPX tracks for the routes in this guide are available to download free at www.cicerone.co.uk/1090/GPX. A GPS device is an excellent aid to navigation, but you should also carry a map and compass and know how to use them. GPX files are provided in good faith, but in view of the profusion of formats and devices, neither the author nor the publisher accepts responsibility for their use.

The ÖAV printed maps are available in digital form on a USB memory stick and can be downloaded to handheld GPS systems. Most refuges publish their GPS co-ordinates on their websites and a complete list is published in the ÖAV Hütten guide. Many signposts show GPS co-ordinates.

ACCOMMODATION

Places to stay overnight on the Adlerweg vary from basic mountain refuges to five-star hotels. In general, you will need to stay in refuges when in the mountains, while on evenings when the path leads down into the valleys, you will find a variety of bed & breakfasts, guesthouses, inns and hotels. Such a network of accommodation means that the need to camp is rare and there are very few official camping sites. A tent is not needed as you are never more than a day's walk from accommodation, and usually only half a day.

Mountain refuges

Austrian mountains are well served by a network of serviced mountain walkers' refuges, called *Hütten* (sing. *Hütte*) in German. Refuges are either operated by the Austrian (ÖAV) or German (DAV) Alpenverein (alpine clubs) or are privately run. On or near the Adlerweg there are 22 Alpenverein refuges and 14 private ones.

Alpine club refuges are owned and managed by individual sections of the Alpenverein, and this is often reflected in their names, such as Erfurter Hütte and Ulmer Hütte. The UK section has no refuges of its own, but members are encouraged to contribute to a fund that helps maintain some of the less well-funded refuges. On the Adlerweg, Steinseehütte in the Lechtaler Alpen has been a beneficiary of this fund, which has contributed to the installation of solar heating and warm showers.

Refuges are graded according to their facilities, and this is reflected in the overnight price. Accommodation can be in individual rooms sleeping from two to eight, or in the slightly cheaper *Lager*, a mixed-sex dormitory often in the roof space. Discounts of

Falkenhütte (photo: Tirol Werbung; photographer – Dominik Gigler) (Stage 9)

at least €12 on accommodation (not food) are given to ÖAV members and members of other national alpine clubs. Most refuges have hot water and many have hot showers for which there is a small charge. Blankets or duvets and pillows are provided, but guests are expected to provide their own sleeping sheet and pillowcase. Self-catering is not usually possible, except at Ackerlhütte (Stage 1) and Loreahütte (Stage 17), which are not serviced.

A central booking system, the Online Hütte Reservation System (OHRS) has been established. At present about 50% of AV refuges participate in the OHRS, but numbers are growing. Refuges that are members of this scheme will not accept direct bookings. The system can be accessed either from the website of individual refuges, through the hut-finder page on the ÖAV website, or via the tour portal www.alpenvereinaktiv.com. Up to 90% of beds are available for reservation, with the rest held back to accommodate late arrivals. At weekends in high season, some refuges, particularly those in the Karwendel, can be very busy. During this period, spare mattresses and put-me-up beds can fill the dining rooms and corridors. Overall, AV refuges offer a warm, welcoming and good value place to eat and sleep.

Most private refuges offer similar facilities and services to AV refuges. Rooms may be a little less spartan and prices slightly higher with no discounts available to AV members. In two locations (Mauritzalm, Stage 7, and Hallerangeralm, Stage 11) private and AV refuges stand in close proximity to each other, giving walkers a choice. It is recommended that AV members use the AV refuge, while non-members should take the private option.

Hotels, inns, guesthouses, bed & breakfasts and youth hostels

Off the mountains, in the towns and villages and in the valleys, you will need to stay in commercial accommodation. Virtually all accommodation is vetted and graded by local tourist organisations, and bookings can be made through local tourist offices.

Hotels tend to be full-service establishments with all facilities (restaurant, bar, sauna, gym and perhaps a pool). Inns, often called *Haus* (although this term can also refer to some mountain refuges) are simpler, often in remote locations, and usually have a restaurant. Guesthouses (*Gasthofen*) sometimes have a restaurant, but not always. B&Bs are private houses that take overnight guests. They have no restaurant but do provide breakfast. They can usually be identified by a sign saying *Zimmer frei* (room available). Inns, guesthouses and B&Bs can all offer very good value and are sometimes no more expensive than mountain refuges. Prices usually include breakfast. There are three *Jugendherbergen* (youth hostels) on the Adlerweg: two in Innsbruck (Stage 12) and one in Igls (Stage 13).

Most non-mountain stage-end places have a variety of accommodation options. For locations such as Schiesti, Pinegg, Fernstein and Boden, where there is no refuge and only one private guest house/inn/hotel, reservations are recommended, particularly at weekends.

Camping

Much of the route is through protected areas where wild camping is prohibited. Wild camping is possible in a few places, but in general the availability of affordable mountain accommodation means very few Adlerweg walkers choose to camp. There are only six official campsites en route, plus six others a short distance away.

Campsites en route are at Langkampfen, Maurach, Lermoos and Fernstein, plus Häselgehr and Elbigenalp on the Lechtal valley alternative. Campsites off-route can be found at St Johann, Kufstein, Innsbruck, Scharnitz, Leutasch and Ehrwald.

FOOD AND DRINK

Places to eat

The Adlerweg is well served by places where walkers can find food and beverages. With the exception of the two non-serviced self-catering huts, all the refuges on the trail provide lunch, and those with accommodation serve breakfast and dinner. In addition, there are a number of *Almhütten* (pasture huts) providing lunchtime fare. All towns and villages on the

Evening in a busy refuge, Karwendelhaus (Stages 10 and 11)

route have places selling food and drink; even tiny hamlets like Engalm (Stage 9) and Boden (Stage 19) have *Gaststätten* (taverns).

Refuges generally offer a choice of hot and cold meals for lunch and dinner, the variety, range and price depending upon the size, popularity and accessibility of the refuge. Most have vehicular or goods-lift access, although some (most notably Anhalter Hütte at the end of Stage 18) need supplies to be carried at least part way. Food is normally of the hearty/ filling variety rather than gourmet cuisine. An inclusive three-course set dinner with accommodation and breakfast is available (often only to prebooked AV members) in some refuges. Many establishments offer their own specialities, but as these depend upon particular wardens, who may change from year to year, they are not listed in this guide. Up-to-date information can usually be obtained from each refuge's website or from the ÖAV Hütten guide. In the past, specialities have included such things as free-range turkey, locally reared beef, game, Italian food, home-made cakes and even Nepalese cooking.

Almhütten (pasture huts) provide a more limited lunchtime fare. Usually operated by the local farmer as a side venture, they typically serve *Jausen* (cold meats, ham, cheese with bread and pickles) accompanied by fresh milk, fresh apple juice and other beverages. Produce is often home-grown or reared. Opening hours are more limited than in refuges, with some opening weekends only, except in high season.

A restaurant usually indicates a slightly more formal environment, with uniformed servers and starched table linen, whereas a *Gaststätte* is generally a more relaxed local eatery. A *Speisesaal* is a dining room, usually within a hotel or guesthouse, while a *Stube* is a dining room decorated in traditional style. An *Imbisstube* is a snack bar.

With the exception of a few upmarket establishments in Innsbruck, meal prices in local restaurants are comparable with the prices in refuges (they do not have the added costs of transportation and live-in labour). A wide range of Tyrolean, Austrian and international food is available. Many restaurants, but not all, have menus available in English. When you want to settle up, you can either say, *zahlen bitte?* (can I pay, please?) or ask for *die Rechnung* (the bill). Tipping is not expected in Austrian restaurants, but it is customary to leave your small change.

Austrian/German food

Although the Adlerweg is entirely in Austria, many refuges are operated by German AV sections and some can only be supplied from the north (Bavarian) side of the mountains. The food and beverages you will encounter will thus be a mix of Tyrolean and Bavarian cuisine.

Refuges usually offer two choices of *Frühstück* (breakfast): simple continental (bread, butter, jam and tea/coffee) or a larger version that also includes cold meats and cheese. Boiled eggs may be available and sometimes fruit juice and breakfast cereals. In refuges, breakfast usually starts from 07:00.

Gröstl, Tyrolean pork and potato hash

Mittagessen (lunch) from 12:00 is the main meal of an Austrian day, although walkers often choose a lighter lunch, with the main meal in the evening. A typical Austrian snack, which may be taken from mid-morning until mid-afternoon, is a *Jause*: a thick slice of bread topped with *Käse* (cheese) or *Schinken* (ham). A more substantial version, consisting of a selection of meats or cheeses and bread (rather like a ploughman's lunch), is served on a wooden platter and known as a *Brettjause*. Other popular lunchtime snacks include *Schinken-Käse-Toast* (ham and cheese toastie) or *Wurst mit Senf*: a plate of sausages and mustard served with *Brot* (bread). Soups include *Gulaschsuppe* (thick beef soup flavoured with paprika), clear broths with strips of pancake and cream soups such as *Knoblauch* (garlic) or *Zweibel* (onion).

Kuchen (cakes), which are often *hausgemacht* (home-made), accompany coffee during the afternoon. Typical Austrian cakes include *Sachertorte*, a chocolate and apricot creation that originated in the Hotel Sacher in Vienna but which can now be found almost anywhere. If you want to try the original recipe, Café Sacher has a branch in the entrance to the Hofburg in Innsbruck, which you pass on Stage 12A.

For *Abendessen* (evening meal), the mainstays of Tyrolean cooking are simple hearty dishes of meat and various kinds of savoury *Knödel* (dense, tennis-ball-sized dumplings),

Kartoffeln (potatoes) or *Spätzle* (noodles). The most common meat is from the pig (pork, gammon, bacon, ham), but you will also find beef or veal, chicken, turkey and occasionally lamb. Austria's most renowned dish, *Wiener schnitzel* (veal escalope fried in egg and breadcrumbs) is almost ubiquitous. Another Austrian speciality is *Tafelspitz* (braised beef). Particularly Tyrolean is *Gröstl*, a hash made from leftover cooked pork, diced potatoes and onions fried in butter and topped with a fried egg. Hunting, which is widely practised in local forests, provides game such as *Reh* (venison), *Gams* (chamois) and *Wildschwein* (wild boar), while anglers catch *Forelle* (trout) from the rivers and *Zander* (pikeperch) from the lakes. The most common vegetable is *Sauerkraut* (pickled cabbage). Abendessen starts at 18:00 in some refuges but is more typically from 19:00.

The most common dessert is *Strudel*, usually apple but sometimes *Marille* (apricot), *Mohn* (poppy seed) or *Topfen* (curd cheese). Two typically Tyrolean, and very substantial, desserts are *Germknödel*, a sweet dumpling filled with poppy seeds and plum jam, served with custard (vanilla sauce), and *Kaiserschmarrn*, a pancake made with raisins, which is served chopped and dusted with sugar.

Vegetarianism is still considered by many Austrians to be an exotic fad, and catering for vegetarians is rather

Parseierspitze, on the horizon, reflected in Mittlerer Seewisee lake (Stage 21)

hit and miss. In refuges, vegetarian fare is unlikely to be more than pasta with tomato sauce, *Knödel* in cheese sauce or a veggie casserole.

Drinks

Tap water is usually safe to drink, and on the few occasions when it is not, you will always be advised *nicht Trinkwasser* (not drinking water). Water in refuges often comes straight from mountain springs. Many drinking fountains and water troughs, often drawing water from springs, can be found along the path, particularly at lower and middle levels. However, as the underlying rock is mostly porous limestone, natural water sources at higher altitudes are often scarce and you should always take water with you.

All the usual soft drinks (colas, lemonade, juices) are widely available. Austrian specialities include *Almdudler*, a drink made from mountain herbs and tasting of elderflower, often used as a mixer with white wine; *Apfelgespritz* or *Apfelschorle*, a blend of apple juice and sparkling water; and *Schiwasser*, raspberry syrup diluted with water. Pasture huts often sell *Milch* (milk) straight from the dairy, although the milk in refuges is usually UHT.

Tyrol, like nearby Bavaria, is a beer-consuming region and beer is available from a wide variety of local and national breweries. Many refuges, except those in the most remote locations, have both bottled and draught beer. The main types of beer are German-style lagers and *Hefeweizen* (wheat beer). Wheat beer popularity is increasing and can be found in both *helles* (pale) and *dunkles* (dark) varieties. Very refreshing and slightly sweet tasting, wheat beer is unfiltered and thus naturally cloudy in appearance. Beer is sold in a number of standard measures: *Pfiff* (200mm), *Kleines* or *Seidel* (300mm) and *Grosses* or *Halbe* (half litre). *Hefeweizen* is traditionally served in half litre, vase-shaped glasses.

A *Radler* (shandy, a blend of beer and lemonade) is a popular and refreshing drink that is always available and, having only 50% of the alcohol content of beer is probably a better choice at lunchtime. *Apfelwein* and *Most* (cider), made from apples, can also be found.

Austria is a major wine-producing country, although almost all Austrian wine comes from the eastern part of the country, with little or no production in Tyrol. Most of the wine produced is white, with *grüner veltliner* the most commonly used grape, along with riesling, *müller-thurgau*, *weissburgunder* and *ruländer*. Red wine, mostly produced from *blauburgunder* (pinot noir) or *rotburger* (zweigelt) grapes, is growing in popularity. Imported, mostly Italian, wines are readily available and often cheaper than Austrian wine. This is not surprising as Italian wine-producing regions are closer to Tyrol than Austrian vineyards. Wine can be bought by the bottle or as *offene Wein* (house wine) by the glass or carafe in *Achtel* (125ml), *Viertel* (250ml), *halbe* (half litre) and litre.

At the close of a meal, Austrians typically drink schnapps, a distillation of alcohol from a wide variety of fruits, berries and herbs. Tyrol is a major producer of fruit schnapps

TYROLEAN FRUIT SCHNAPPS

There is a particularly wide selection of schnapps at Tuxerbauer distillery in Tulfes, near the bottom of the Glungezerbahn cable car (Stage 13). Schnapps makes an excellent souvenir but is not very practical to carry around. However, as Tulfes is only a short bus trip from Innsbruck, you could always return at the end of your walk and pick up a bottle or two before travelling home.

Tyrolean fruit schnapps

(typically about 40% alcohol) and fruit liqueurs (less strong at about 20%). Small local suppliers often produce these (there are 20,000 registered schnapps distilleries in Austria) from fruits such as *Williamsbirnen* (pears), *Marillen* (apricots), *Zwetschgen* (plums), and *myrtilles* (bilberries). Particularly distinctive tastes are those of *Krauter*, a distillation flavoured with herbs, and *Enzian*, which is distilled from the root of the gentian flower. Schnapps is usually bottled commercially, although sometimes you will find local distillations decanted into unmarked bottles. Many refuges have a *haus schnaps*, sometimes home produced. Beware, quality and strength can vary greatly from sophisticated smoothness to throat-burning firewater!

Coffee is the Austrian hot drink of choice. Legend has it that coffee was introduced in 1683 when retreating Ottoman troops left bags of beans behind after the Battle of Vienna. Coffee is served in a wide variety of styles. *Mokka* or *kleiner Schwarzer* (small black) is similar to espresso; *kleiner Brauner* (small brown) is served with milk; *Verlängerter* (lengthened) is diluted with hot water; *Melange* (mixed) is topped up with hot milk; while *Einspänner* is topped with whipped cream. Italian styles such as cappuccino and café latte are also commonly served.

Tea is growing in popularity. *Schwarzer Tee* (black tea or English breakfast tea) is widely available,

along with a range of fruit and herbal teas. Tea is served with lemon. If you want it with cold milk, you need to ask for *Tee mit kalt Milch*. To warm yourself up on a cold day you could try hot chocolate with rum, a popular winter après-ski drink.

AMENITIES AND SERVICES

Shops

All towns and larger villages on the route have grocery stores, often small supermarkets and many have pharmacies. Opening hours vary, but most open early. Grocery stores close at 13:00 on Saturdays and stay closed all day Sunday. Clothing and outdoor equipment stores can be found in St Johann, Kufstein, Pertisau, Innsbruck, Leutasch, Ehrwald, Lermoos, Elbigenalp and St Anton.

Post offices

All towns and some villages have post offices. Opening hours vary.

Currency and banks

Austria changed from using *Schillings* to Euros in 2002. There are banks in St Johann, Kufstein, Unterlangkampfen, Maurach, Pertisau, Innsbruck, Igls, Weidach, Ehrwald, Lermoos, Elbigenalp, Häselgehr, Holzgau, Steeg and St Anton. Normal opening hours are 08:00–12:30 and 13:30–15:00 (weekdays only), with extended opening until 17:30 on Thursdays. Most branches have ATM machines, which

The Adlerweg ascends across screes towards Grossbergspitze (Stage 21)

enable you to make transactions in English. Contact your bank before you leave home to activate your card for use in Austria.

Telephones

Austria has extensive *Handy* (mobile phone) coverage, even in mountain areas, where signals can often be received from the valleys below. Contact your network provider before you leave home to ensure your phone is enabled for foreign use and that you have the optimum price package. If you plan to make many local calls once you have arrived, it usually pays to obtain a local SIM card. The

international dialling code for Austria is +43, although some DAV refuges are contacted via Germany using +49.

Most hotels and guesthouses, plus refuges if they have a signal, provide free Wi-Fi access to guests.

Electricity

Voltage is 220v, 50HzAC. Plugs are standard European two-pin round.

WHAT TO TAKE

Clothing

On a two-or-three-week traverse of the Adlerweg it is necessary to plan for a wide range of climatic conditions and dress accordingly. But remember, you have to carry everything on your back and weight is at a premium (a good maxim is 'one to wear, one to wash'). The best way to cope with this is to carry multiple thin layers: T-shirt, short-sleeved shirt, long-sleeved shirt, roll-neck, sweater or fleece, under-wear, shorts, lightweight long trousers, plus waterproof jacket and over-trousers to protect against wind and rain. Two good pairs of walking socks plus lining socks are essential. All of this clothing should be easy to wash en route, and a small tube or bottle of travel wash is useful. Drying can be achieved overnight (most refuges have drying rooms) or by hanging clothes on your backpack the next day (take a few large safety pins). Accessories should include a sun hat for hot days and a woolly hat and lightweight gloves for cold ones.

The going underfoot is usually dry and a good pair of summer light-weight walking boots should suffice. Boots should be 'worn-in' but with good tread depth to provide grip on slippery rocks, scree slopes and late-season snow. Most refuges provide slippers, as boots are prohibited in sleeping accommodation, but train-ers are useful when overnighting elsewhere.

The route below Laliderer Wände, with Falkenhütte on the grassy ridge and Birkkarspitze behind (Stage 9)

Equipment

A good quality weather resistant backpack is essential. The maximum size should be 40 litres (60 litres in the unlikely event you choose to carry camping gear). No matter how weather resistant the pack, persistent rain always finds a way through, but a thick plastic inner liner, such as a rubble sack, available from builders' merchants, will prevent the contents from getting wet. Anything carried in side or top pockets should be waterproofed with individual plastic freezer bags.

Almost every walker nowadays carries one or two telescopic walking poles. These are particularly useful on steep descents and on unstable ground such as scree. In early season, before mid July on the highest stages, you may wish to carry crampons and an ice axe. For the Lechtaler Alpen stages karabiners might be useful but are not essential.

Good quality sunglasses protect your eyes against the glare from areas of exposed white limestone and snowfields, while a high factor suncream protects exposed skin from strong UV radiation at higher altitudes. Although the Adlerweg is not a high-risk area for insect bites, insect repellent is useful to protect against the normal range of insect predators, as well as soothing lotion for post-bite relief.

For nights in AV refuges, you will need a sleeping sheet. By far the best, although expensive, is a lightweight silk sleeping bag weighing only a few grams and packing into a bag smaller than a pair of socks. You will also need a towel and the usual range of toiletries. A small torch can be useful at night in a crowded dormitory.

En route you will need a compass, this guidebook and a range of maps (ideally with a map case to carry them in). On lower stages, drinking water from springs and fountains is frequently available. However, once above 1500m, ground water becomes scarce and you will need to carry a water bottle. For personal health and safety, you should carry a simple first-aid kit and a whistle.

SAFETY AND SECURITY

Weather

Austria has a continental climate typified by warm, dry summers and cold winters. However, in the western part of the country, including Tyrol, this is moderated by both Atlantic and Mediterranean weather systems. As a result, while summer in Tyrol is generally warmer and drier than Britain, the east–west barrier formed by the Alps has a pronounced climatic effect. West or north-west winds can bring cool damp Atlantic air masses to the region, causing clouds to form over the northern slopes. As a result, the Germany-facing north side of the mountains is cooler and wetter than the south-facing Inn valley side. Occasional southerly winds from the Mediterranean bring warm, dry weather, including the well-known *Föhn* wind. This wind, originating in the Sahara, can cause temperatures to rise 10°C above normal and is said to cause irritability and headaches.

With Tyrol being a mountainous region, the weather can change greatly from day to day and even within a day. Showers can occur at any time, while heavy thunderstorms are more likely in the evenings. Weather also changes with altitude. Even in midsummer, rain can sometimes fall as sleet or snow above 2000m.

Summer sun can be strong in Tyrol, particularly at altitude, and can even burn through light cloud. An adequate level of sun protection is essential for exposed skin, and a sun hat should be worn. Lip salve can protect lips from both sun and wind.

Most refuges, and some guest-houses and hotels, provide daily internet mountain weather forecasts obtained from the local tourist office. These are usually displayed the evening before and are generally reliable. Austrian mountain weather forecasts from ORF (Austrian state broadcaster) can be found at wetter.orf.at/tirol/bergwetter.

Mountain safety

Care is always necessary when mountain walking and the Adlerweg is no exception. On white and red stages, the going should prove straightforward with few obstacles. However, on black stages there will be some scrambling, and you will encounter

Valluga Grat (2646m) can be reached by cable car from St Anton (Stage 24)

Parseierspitze (L) is the highest point in the Nördliche Kalkalpen, here seen from Grossbergspitze (Stage 21)

cables, pegs and ladders which must be accessed with care. The most common safety threat is from slippery rocks, particularly after rainfall; however, most places where such rocks occur are protected with precautionary fixed cables. After a heavy winter, snow can remain all year in some higher parts of Karwendelgebirge and Lechtaler Alpen, and fresh snow is not unknown, even in August.

Most of the paths are well walked and other walkers are frequently encountered, although one or two stages, including the Köglhörndl ridge (Stage 4) and Haimbachtal (Stage 18), are less visited. Provided you are properly equipped and provisioned, experienced in the use of map and compass, fit enough to cover your planned daily route and have up-to-date weather information and knowledge of accident and emergency procedures, you should have no problems even on the more remote stages. Solo walkers should consider letting someone know their planned daily itinerary. AV refuges usually have a register where you can enter your planned route.

Emergencies

If an accident does occur, help can be summoned in a number of ways.

Traditionally, the international distress call is a series of six blasts on a whistle (or torch flashes after dark) spread over a period of one minute and repeated after one minute's pause. The response is three blasts per minute. To summon help from the air, both arms should be raised above your head in the form of a Y (if help is not required, raise only one arm, keeping the other by your side).

Much of the Adlerweg is covered by mobile phone reception, which combined with GPS technology provides the most effective way of alerting the emergency services. You should call the general emergency number (112), where the operator will ascertain your location and put you through to the local police. The police will decide the best response and connect you with the relevant emergency service, either ambulance or *Bergrettungsdienst* (mountain rescue) or both. As mountain rescue is a voluntary service, it is normal to make a donation after the event to Bergrettungsdienst funds.

The Adlerweg traverses many types of terrain, much of it remote and only accessible on foot. However, apart from the higher parts of Karwendelgebirge and the Lechtaler Alpen, road access for 4WD vehicles is seldom more than a few kilometres away. In areas that are too remote for road access, evacuation is undertaken by helicopter. Emergency helicopter landing places are shown on ÖAV 1:25,000 maps.

Should you require hospital treatment, there are a number of first-class hospitals with A&E departments spread along the Inn valley, all well equipped for dealing with mountain accidents. Provided you have an EHIC card issued by an EU or EEA member state or a British GHIC card, medical costs are covered under reciprocal health insurance arrangements, although you may have to pay for an ambulance and claim the cost back through insurance.

Travel insurance policies usually cover mountain walking, provided you are not using specialist equipment such as ropes, karabiners or ice axes – but check the small print. If you are a member of ÖAV (recommended), emergency rescue, hospital and repatriation costs are covered by their insurance.

ABOUT THIS GUIDE

All 24 stages, plus the 3-stage Lechtal valley alternative route, which avoids the black stages of the Lechtaler Alpen, are described in full in this guide, including details of all locations where meals, refreshments and/or lodgings are available, plus a few other locations close by. Stages are grouped into sections, each covering a particular geographic area. The abbreviation 'sp' for 'signpost' is used throughout.

Timings are based on a fit walker carrying a moderate pack in good weather conditions and walking the

The Goetheweg crossing the Nordkette summit ridge at Mühlkarscharte, with a view of Innsbruck in the Inntal valley below (photo: Tirol Werbung; photographer – Hans Herbig) (Stage 12)

stage without stopping. Appendix A provides walking times and distances between intermediate reference points. Taken in conjunction with the suggested 16-day and 21-day schedules, it can be used to plan your own timetable. Remember to allow ample time to reach each night's accommodation. Average speeds required to meet these timings range from less than 1kph in difficult terrain to between 4 and 5kph on flat country roads. Grades of difficulty are taken from those published by local tourist bodies.

Published altitudes can vary. This guide uses altitudes as they appear on ÖAV maps. These may differ from those found on the outside of refuges, which may reflect earlier measurements before accurate satellite mapping became available.

In the descriptions of refuge facilities, the total number of permanent summer beds is shown, with an indication of how many are in bedrooms (b) and dormitories (d). Details of facilities available and opening and closing times were correct at the time of going to press but will change over time.

Even the path is subject to change. Rockfalls and washouts cause blockages and diversions, some of which become permanent. Look out for local signage showing such changes.

Most geographic features incorporate in their names the German term describing them, for example Achensee (Achen lake), Lechtal (Lech valley) and Loreascharte (Lorea notch). In the route descriptions the full German name is used with the English translation added, hence Achensee lake, Lechtal valley and Loreascharte notch, except on the maps, where only the German usage appears.

Mapping is on a scale of 1:50,000. The main Adlerweg route is always shown in red; notwithstanding stages may be classified as white, red or black. Alternative routes described in the text, usually easier route options avoiding black stages, are shown in blue, while purple is used for connecting routes and short off-route excursions. Sections that use cable cars or chairlifts are indicated by a broken line.

THE ROUTE

Looking back to Birkkarspitze from Birkkarklamm gorge (photo: Christine Gordon) (Stage 11)

SECTION 1
KAISERGEBIRGE

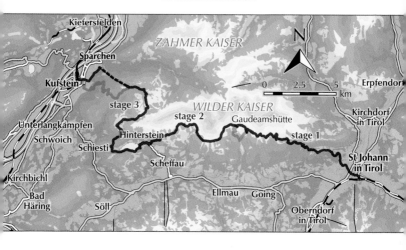

STAGE 1
St Johann in Tirol to Gaudeamushütte

Start	St Johann in Tirol station (670m)
Finish	Gaudeamushütte (1263m)
Distance	13km
Ascent	1100m
Descent	510m
Grade	Red
Time	5hr
Highest point	Baumgartenköpfl (1560m)
Maps	ÖAV8 (1:25,000); FB301 (1:50,000); K09 (1:25,000)
Access	Hourly ÖBB trains between Wörgl and Schwarzach-St Veit call at St Johann
	20min walk from Gaudeamushütte to Wochenbrunneralm for frequent shuttle bus to Ellmau

A quiet country road leads to a forest path climbing through the Niederkaiser foothills to Diebsöfen cave and Schleierwasserfall, where the 60m sheer rock face behind the waterfall is popular with climbers. Emerging above the trees, you get your first close-up views of the jagged Wilder Kaiser peaks. The path crosses the heads of two valleys to reach its highest point at Baumgartenköpfl before descending steeply to Gaudeamushütte with spectacular views of Ellmauer Halt (2344m).

Although the official Adlerweg starts from Rummlerhof, 4km by quiet country road from St Johann in Tirol, the route described here starts at St Johann station.

St Johann in Tirol (all services, accommodation, meals/refreshments, tourist office Poststrasse 2, +43 535 263 3350, www.kitzbueheler-alpen.com, rail and bus stations). From **St Johann station** (670m), go straight ahead along Bahnhofstrasse,

ST JOHANN IN TIROL, KITZBÜHEL'S LESS WELL-KNOWN NEIGHBOUR

Situated in the Leukental valley, between the Kitzbüheler Alps and the Kaisergebirge, St Johann in Tirol gets its name from a church dedicated to St John the Baptist (St Johann in German), which was built by Catholic missionaries before AD738. Copper and silver mines, opened in 1540, ushered in a period of prosperity that lasted until the 18th century. Indeed, in the 17th century the 778m Heilig-Geist-Schacht (Holy Ghost Shaft) was the deepest mine shaft in the world. Throughout this period, St Johann remained a village, while Kitzbühel, just 10km along the valley, prospered as a medieval city, its charter having been granted in 1271.

The coming of the railway in 1875 led to the growth of tourism. With the extensive development of ski runs in the Kitzbüheler Alpen, Kitzbühel became one of the most prominent winter sports resorts in Europe. As Kitzbüheler Horn ski area is equally accessible from both places, St Johann shared in this success, becoming a less expensive alternative to glamorous Kitzbühel. In 1956, St Johann was recognised as a market town and much of the commercial development since then has taken place there. Indeed, the population of St Johann (9400) now exceeds that of Kitzbühel (8300).

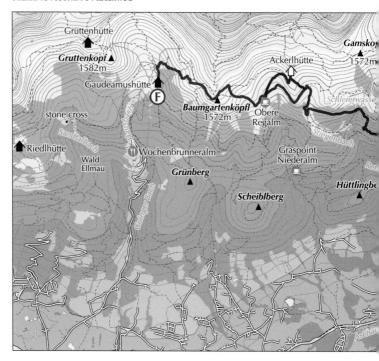

passing the hospital L. Bear L at a roundabout, still following Bahnhofstrasse, to reach the town square, Hauptplatz, with the parish church R. Cross the square and exit far L opposite the post office. This short street leads to Kaiserstrasse where you turn R. If you turn L, the tourist office is second building L. Continue along Kaiserstrasse, crossing the **Kitzbüheler Ache** river. Bear R at a

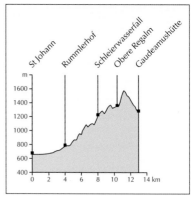

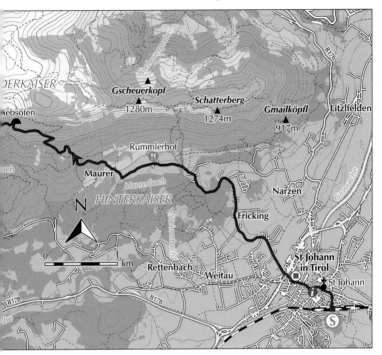

fork (sp Hinterkaiserweg), passing the bus station R, to reach the main road at a roundabout (**10min**).

Cross the roundabout and leave St Johann by Hinterkaiserweg (sp Adlerweg), which you follow for 3km, ignoring all side roads. The road bends L and R, sometimes quite sharply. Level at first through meadows and occasional houses, it begins to ascend gently after **Fricking** as you reach the trees. Ahead you can see the Niederkaiser ridge, with the bare limestone of the much higher Wilder Kaiser rising beyond. Looking back there is a good view of the Kitzbüheler Horn (1996m) above St Johann. Shortly before reaching Rummlerhof, cross a cattle grid where there is a sign L officially marking the start of the Adlerweg. A row of large boulders accompanying the sign carries the names of the various mountain ranges passed by on the route. Hinterkaiserweg passes **Rummlerhof** R (780m) (meals/refreshments, Apr–Oct, closed Mon) (**40min**).

From Rummlerhof, continue along Hinterkaiserweg for 750 metres, bearing R to reach **Maurer** (818m), where the road ends. Pass the farmhouse R and turn immediately R (sp Schleierwasserfall) beside a water trough onto a grassy path which ascends through meadows towards the woods. Cross a stile and continue winding up through the trees. Go ahead over a second stile and continue uphill, eventually crossing a stream by a wooden bridge and bearing R onto a 4WD track. Continue uphill to reach a forestry road at a sharp bend and turn L. After 25 metres turn R, still uphill, onto a smaller forestry road. When this ends, turn R uphill on a path through the trees. At a path junction, bear L then after 125 metres turn R on a path uphill. Follow this round two zigzags then at a third zigzag continue ahead contouring for 700 metres, with a short section along a cliff face, where a steep drop-off has fixed cables for security, to reach **Diebsöfen** cave (1086m) (**1hr 20min**).

You are now below steep cliffs with a huge open-fronted cavern eroded into them. Follow the path as it descends for a short way through the cavern. The floor of the cave is very uneven and very slippery. Above your head, the cavern roof is one of Europe's most difficult 'dry tool' climbing pitches. Looking up, you can see pitons and karabiners left by previous visitors.

Continuing below the line of cliffs, a winding ascent brings you to the impressive **Schleierwasserfall** (1158m). The water tumbles down cliffs with a 60m drop, the path running through the eroded cavern behind the falls (**30min**). The waterfall is a popular climbing location and climbers are often seen inching their way up the precarious cliffs behind and beside the falls.

Walkers have to pass behind the water at Schleierwasserfall

The cliffs beside Schleierwasserfall are a popular climbing location

From the falls, continue on a path, passing a toilet hut R, scrambling up boulders beside the cliffs (sp Gaudeamushütte) for a further 750 metres, then descend into a coomb below Stiegenbachwasserfall. At the bottom of the coomb bear L then turn sharply R (sp Ackerlhütte) and ascend the other side to reach meadows above the cliffs. From here, the jagged peaks of Ackerlspitze (2329m) and its neighbours come into view ahead. Continue through meadows, ascending in a long arc, curving round from initially heading NE and ending up heading SW, to reach the top of a ridge at Ackerlrucken.

From Ackerlrucken, an easy walk along a grassy ridge takes you to **Ackerlhütte** (1465m), which can be seen R about 400 metres away and 100m above (ÖAV, 15 beds 0b/15d, self-catering, open mid May–end Oct, warden at weekends only, AV key required at other times, +43 664 254 2503, **www.alpenverein.at/kitzbuehel**) (15min off-route).

The path descends into another grassy coomb, with the path curving L to reach **Obere Regalm** pasture hut (1315m) (snacks/refreshments, early Jun–early Oct, Wed/Sat/Sun 10:00–17:00) (**1hr**).

53

Leave by a path ascending through meadows behind the refuge (sp Gaudeamushütte), following waymarks painted on occasional rocks. At a painted arrow, turn sharply R and continue ascending NW through a coomb to reach a junction with a path coming directly from Ackerlhütte. Turn L and contour to reach the day's high point (1560m) below **Baumgartenköpfl**, with a summit cross above the path L (**35min**).

Descend slowly on a path winding through dwarf conifers past Freiberghaus, where a magnificent view appears. On a ridge across the valley is Gruttenhütte, and towering above it are the spires and peaks of Ellmauer Halt (2344m), the highest point in the Kaisergebirge. Descend steeply into the valley, zigzagging through the trees before bearing L to reach **Gaudeamushütte** (1263m) (DAV, 48 beds 32b/16d, meals/refreshments, mid May–mid Oct, +43 5358 2262, www. dav-main-spessart.at) (**45min**).

DER KAISERGEBIRGE: THE CLIMBERS' MOUNTAINS

The mountains north and south of St Johann could not be more different. The Kitzbüheler Alpen, seen to the left throughout the first two stages, are rounded and green, and being the site of one of Europe's finest skiing areas, they are well developed. The Kaisergebirge, towering above on your right, are jagged, rocky and white and contain many challenging climbing routes and *Klettersteig* (via ferrata). Tourist infrastructure is limited to a few mountain refuges.

This difference in development lies in a referendum held in 1961, which resulted in the Kaisergebirge being declared a protected area. Plans to develop the skiing industry were blocked. As a result, only one man-made up-lift exists in the range, the Kaiserlift chairlift at Brentenjoch, which the Adlerweg uses to descend to Kufstein at the end of Stage 3. The range consists of two mountain blocks: the high, wild and jagged Wilder Kaiser (Wild Emperor) and the slightly lower Zahmer Kaiser (Tame Emperor), divided by the Kaisertal valley.

The Wilder Kaiser Steig (WKS) long-distance path loops around the Wilder Kaiser on a four-day circuit from Kirchdorf. For most of Stages 1 and 2 it parallels the Adlerweg, contouring around the mountains at a higher altitude. The WKS is a more challenging route than the Adlerweg, with more height gain and some sections of Klettersteig.

STAGE 2
Gaudeamushütte to Schiesti (Hintersteinersee)

Start	Gaudeamushütte (1263m)
Finish	Schiesti (Hintersteinersee) (922m)
Distance	14.5km
Ascent	800m
Descent	1140m
Grade	Mostly red, but the Klamml ascent to Gruttenhütte is black
Time	6hr
Highest point	Gruttenhütte (1620m)
Maps	ÖAV8 (1:25,000); FB301 (1:50,000); K09 (1:25,000)
Access	Frequent shuttle bus from Ellmau to Wochenbrunneralm, then 20min walk to Gaudeamushütte
	Frequent shuttle bus from Hintersteinersee to Scheffau

After a steep assisted climb to Gruttenhütte, this stage becomes a mid-level walk on forest and meadow paths contouring well below the Wilder Kaiser summits before descending to Hintersteinersee lake, a popular tourist spot, where it is possible to cool off with a refreshing swim.

The stage starts with a very steep, difficult and partially assisted ascent, which is graded black, from Gaudeamushütte through the Klamml gorge to Gruttenhütte. As the path up the gorge is liable to closure due to rockfalls, you should check at the refuge if the path is open before setting off. An alternative route drops down a little from Gaudeamushütte, then follows the Gruttenweg up through forest.

Klamml route to Gruttenhütte
From **Gaudeamushütte** head NNW (sp Gruttenhütte über Klamml) across meadows, on a path that crosses a river washout (often dry by midsummer) and ascends through scrub towards the col R of **Gruttenkopf**. This narrow path

gains height as it ascends a valley through dwarf conifers and scrub with the Hausbach stream L. Cross the stream in a narrow defile to enter Klamml gorge. The section through the gorge is aided by fixed cables, bolted hand/footholds and a 3m ladder. Above the gorge, join the Gruttenweg trail to soon reach **Gruttenhütte** (1620m) (DAV, 97 beds 79b/18d, meals/refreshments, early Jun–mid Oct, +43 5358 43389, www.grutten-huette.at) (**1hr 30min**).

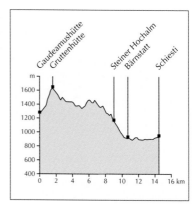

Alternative route avoiding Klamml

From **Gaudeamushütte** head SW (sp Wochenbrunneralm) on a 4WD track. Cross the Hausbach stream and continue parallel with it for 900 metres to reach a path junction (1137m). Fork R (sp Riedlhütte) on a path ascending into the forest. If you

continue ahead for 500 metres, you reach Wochenbrunneralm (meals/refreshments, bus to Ellmau). After 200 metres, the path reaches Gruttenweg (**20min**). Turn sharply R (sp Gruttenhütte) then bear L after 100 metres to follow a winding path uphill through the trees. Above the forest, continue through dwarf conifers, scrub and scree, with some easy scrambling over rough stone. Eventually, Gruttenhütte comes into sight above L as the path passes below some masts on the top of **Gruttenkopf**. On the col, the Klamml path from Gaudeamushütte comes in R and the combined route continues a short distance to **Gruttenhütte** (1620m) (**1hr 10min**).

Combined route continues

Follow the 4WD track that sweeps downhill W from the refuge. This is part of the Wilder Kaiser Steig (WKS), which is followed as far as Steiner Hochalm. It is waymarked with yellow paint flashes. After 1.2km fork R (sp Hintersteinersee), leaving the 4WD track but staying on the WKS. The track undulates gently through dwarf conifers and trees, crossing occasional tongues of scree, round the base of Treffauer (2304m), which rises steeply above the trees R. Pass a faint path R that leads to the summit of Tuxegg. After 2.5km, a path comes in L from the valley below (**1hr**).

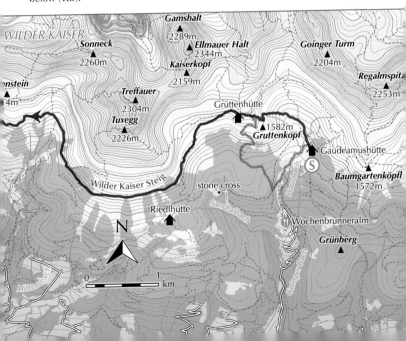

The path curves round to the L, with a yellow arrow and painted WKS showing the way uphill. Fixed cables protect a short section leading up onto a ridge. Fork L at a junction, where a path R ascends to the summit of Treffauer, and pass through an area with a number of huge boulders, some the size of a house, which have fallen from the mountains above. Continue through dwarf conifers and scrub and emerge into meadows at **Kaiser Hochalm**, where there are a group of barns and shepherds' refuges (1417m) (**45min**).

Descend across the meadows, picking up a 4WD track to the SW that first bears R and then back L (sp Hintersteinersee). Pass through a gate and enter broadleaf woodland. After 1km, the 4WD track turns L. At this point continue ahead on a path descending through the trees. This comes out above a new 4WD track. Turn R on a path uphill alongside a fence and L through a gate to cross grassy slopes and arrive at **Steiner Hochalm** pasture hut (1257m) (snacks/refreshments, open all day) (**45min**).

To continue directly to **Walleralm**, avoiding the descent to Hintersteinersee, you can stay on the WKS, which contours through the woods from Steiner Hochalm around the base of Scheffauer. This path rises and falls gently, passing a number of enormous termite mounds, some almost 2m high. Far below, through the trees to the L, you catch frequent glimpses of Hintersteinersee. Cross a number of scree tongues and washouts, and after 3km start descending steeply through scrub and into meadows to join Stage 3 at Walleralm, where accommodation is available.

Leave Steiner Hochalm past barns (sp Hintersteinersee) and turn L on an eroded path descending steeply SW through trees. Bear L to reach a junction with a little-used and badly eroded mule/4WD track. Turn R and follow this track, cutting down between eroded and partially overgrown hairpins as the track descends. The track quality improves and becomes a 4WD track, continuing downhill. After a sharp bend L, turn R off the track (sp Bärnstatt), past houses and through a car park, to reach a surfaced road by St Leonhard Kapelle L and **Gasthaus Bärnstatt** (918m) (30 beds 30b/0d, meals/refreshments, +43 5358 8113, **www.baernstatt. at**) (**45min**).

Turn R and follow the surfaced road for 1km to the shore of Hintersteinersee lake (892m), and **Gasthof Seestüberl** (accommodation, meals/refreshments, closed Tue, +43 5358 8191, **www.seestueberl.info**) (**15min**).

Pass a car park L and turn L opposite the Gasthof to reach the lakeside. Dogleg L and R to cross Hintersteiner Seebach stream and follow a path winding through

Hintersteinersee

woods. The obvious path over the dam at the head of the lake is private and cannot be used; take the first bridge downstream instead. Turn sharply R at first path junction and continue on the path, now rising slightly above the lake. Emerge into a meadow and turn R past houses R. Fork R back into woods and follow the Seespitz track parallel with the lakeshore R. Continue beyond the end of the lake and turn R through meadows to reach **Pension Maier** (24 beds 24b/0d, meals/refreshments, +43 5358 8203, **www.pension-maier.at**) in **Schiesti** (922m) (**1hr**).

STAGE 3

Schiesti (Hintersteinersee) to Kufstein

Start	Schiesti (Hintersteinersee) (922m)
Finish	Kufstein (499m)
Distance	11km (16km using Panoramaweg)
Ascent	820m
Descent	510m (1215m using Panoramaweg)
Grade	Red
Time	4hr 10min (5hr using Panoramaweg)
Highest point	Hochegg (1470m)
Maps	ÖAV8 (1:25,000), FB301 (1:50,000), K09 (1:25,000)
Access	Frequent shuttle bus from Scheffau to Hintersteinersee
	Train from Kufstein to Innsbruck, Munich, Salzburg

This short stage climbs over the western tip of the Wilder Kaiser using a mixture of vehicular tracks and paths through forest and alpine meadows. Dropping down past the hamlet of Steinbergalm, the route crosses a gorge before climbing again to end at the top station of the Kaiserlift chairlift, which the Adlerweg uses to reach Kufstein. Alternatively, the Panoramaweg can be followed downhill into the town.

From **Schiesti**, take the good quality gravel 4WD track N past a car park and follow it as it ascends round two hairpin bends and into forest. Continue on the winding track, ignoring all turns to L or R, with level sections interspersed between short steep ascents. On one of the hairpin bends you get an excellent first view L of the Inn valley with the Brandenberg mountains rising behind. These mountains are visited on the next two stages. Eventually, you reach the little settlement of Stöfflalm (1148m)

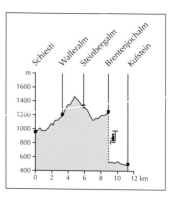

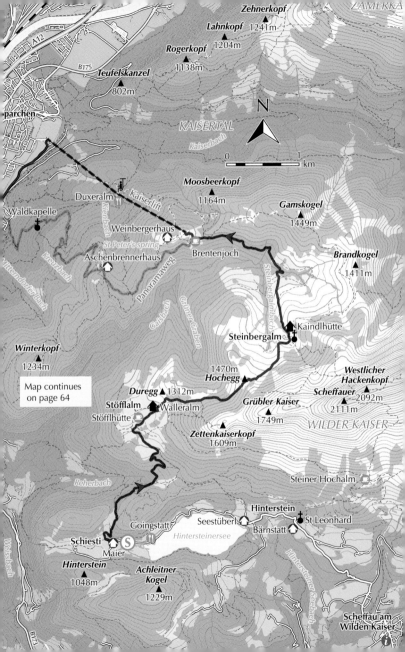

Zehnerkopf

Lahnkopf
1241m
1204m

Rogerkopf
1138m

Teufelskanzel
802m

parchen

A12

B175

KAISERTAL

Kaiserbach

N

0   1
km

Moosbeerkopf
1164m

Gamskogel
1449m

Duxeralm

Kaiserlift

Waldkapelle

Weinbergerhaus

St Peter's spring

Brentenjoch

Brandkogel
1411m

Aschenbrennerhaus

Panoramaweg

Kraudachbach

Wittendorfer Bach

Grüner Graben

Gatzbach

Steinbergalmbach

Kaindlhütte

Steinbergalm

Winterkopf
1234m

Map continues
on page 64

1470m
Hochegg

*Westlicher
Hackenkopf*
2092m

Scheffauer
2111m

Grübler Kaiser
1749m

Duregg ▲ 1342m

Stöfflalm

Walleralm

Stöfflhütte

Zettenkaiserkopf
1609m

WILDER KAISER

Reherbach

Steiner Hochalm

Wetschach

Hintersteinersee

Hinterstein

Seestüberl

St Leonhard

Bärnstatt

Goingstatt

S

Schiesti

Maier

Hinterstein
1048m

*Achleitner
Kogel*
1229m

Hintersteiner Seebach

B73

Scheffau am
Wilden Kaiser

where there is **Stöfflhütte** pasture hut (snacks/refreshments, May–Oct, closed Mon). A short distance further is **Alpengasthof Walleralm** (1172m) (19 beds 19b/0d, booking recommended especially at weekends, meals/refreshments, mid Apr–early Nov, +43 664 985 8139, **www.walleralm.eu**) (**1hr 15min**).

At Walleralm, pass the refuge L and turn L (sp Kaindlhütte) on a rough path that leads NE across meadows, following painted stone waymarks. Bear R at a small col and head uphill following a tongue of grass between the trees. A short section in forest is followed by an ascent through meadows to reach a col beside **Hochegg** summit (1470m) with a hilltop cross L (**1hr**).

From the summit, the path descends through meadows to reach the hamlet of **Steinbergalm**, which can be seen ahead (1293m). In the hamlet is a beautiful white chapel R and the **Kaindlhütte** (private, 47 beds 27b/20d, meals/refreshments, early May–end Oct, booking recommended, +43 5372 21255, **www. kaindlhuette.com**) (**20min**).

Follow a vehicular track NNW. After 500 metres, where the track bends R, continue ahead and drop down through meadows, past the base station of a dismantled chairlift R. The dismantled chairlift previously operated between Brentenjochalm and Steinbergalm. Go ahead (sp Kaiserlift) over a 4WD track to reach the Griesbachklamm gorge. The path drops down into the gorge, crossing the river by a wooden footbridge, then turns sharply L, ascending to regain the vehicular track. Bear L and follow the track contouring along the side of Gamsberg, which rises R, then cross a ford and ascend to Brentenjochalm where the track passes between the top station of the dismantled Steinberg chairlift R and **Brentenjoch** pasture hut (1204m) L (snacks/refreshments, end May–Oct) (**40min**).

At Brentenjoch there is a choice of routes to Kufstein, which lies more than 700m below in the Inn valley. The 'official route' uses the Kaiserlift chairlift to reach Sparchen, an outlying part of Kufstein, while an alternative allows you to walk down following a mix of 4WD vehicular tracks and forest paths for 6.6km on the long and winding Panoramaweg.

To use the Kaiserlift chairlift

Bear R on a faint path winding uphill to reach the chairlift top station (1229m), which can be seen just over the brow (**5min**). Chairlift operates start May–end Oct, 08:30–16:30. Descend to **Obere Sparchen** (501m) (**20min**), which is 1.8km NE of Kufstein town centre.

A single-seater chairlift links Brentenjoch with Kufstein

When the ancient wooden single-seater **Kaiserlift** closed after the 2011 season, many people thought it would never reopen. The cost of renovation and bringing it up to modern standards exceeded the income generated by the operating company. Eventually, Kufstein council stepped in and the renovation went ahead, the lift reopening in 2015. It is still a single-seater chairlift, one of only ten in Austria, but nowadays it has padded seats and modern safety systems. The two-stage journey has an intermediate station at Duxeralm.

At the bottom of the chairlift, turn L in the car park then R onto Energieweg, parallel with cliffs L. Pass a memorial L to Friedrich List (a 19th-century German economist) and further on one on R to Tyrolean patriot Andreas Hofer. Turn R at the end (Kienbergstrasse) then continue ahead (Georg Primoser-Strasse) to reach Unterer Stadtplatz in **Kufstein** town centre (499m) (**30min**) (all services, accommodation, meals/refreshments, tourist office 11–13 Unterer Stadtplatz, +43 5372 62207, **www.kufstein.com**, railway and bus stations).

To walk down using Panoramaweg

Continue ahead on the vehicular track and immediately fork L. The R fork leads steeply uphill and after 350 metres reaches Weinbergerhaus (1273m) (private, 22 beds 22b/0d, meals/refreshments, early May–end Oct, +43 664 256 4760, **www.weinbergerhaus.at**). Continue gently downhill on Panoramaweg, winding through forest to reach **Aschenbrennerhaus** (1135m) (23 beds 23b/0d, early Apr–end Oct, no overnight Sun and Mon nights, meals/refreshments 09:00–18:00, closed Mon, +43 5372 62220, **www.berghaus-aschenbrenner.com**) (**30min**).

Pass below the guest house and follow the track downhill round three hairpins, passing **St Peter's spring** beside the third hairpin. Just before the next hairpin, turn R onto a forest path, then where this crosses the 4WD track, dogleg L and R to continue on the path. Turn R at the next track junction and L at a T-junction, rejoining Panoramaweg. Continue round five hairpins, then at the sixth turn L

63

onto a good forest path. This runs parallel with, but just above, Panoramaweg and passes **Waldkapelle** L (698m) (**45min**).

Keep L to continue on the forest path, then emerge on Panoramaweg and turn L. Pass turning on R (sp *Aussichtsplatz* – viewpoint) and take next turning R (sp Kufstein) steeply downhill through forest. Emerge on Schützenstrasse on the edge of Kufstein and turn L. Bear R over a small bridge then turn L at a T-junction (Kienbergstrasse) and follow this ahead as it becomes Georg Primoser-Strasse to reach Unterer Stadtplatz in the centre of **Kufstein** (499m) (**30min**).

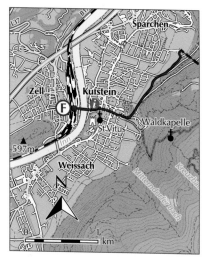

AN UNUSUAL WAR MEMORIAL

At noon every day (and again at 18:00 in July/August) the town centre of Kufstein is filled with the sound of organ music. The Heldenorgel (Heroes' Organ), built in 1931 in memory of the fallen from World War 1, is installed inside the Bürgerturm tower of Kufstein castle. With 46 registers, 4 manuals and 4300 pipes, it is the largest organ of its type in the world. Its position just under the roof of the fortress gives it unusual resonance that, with favourable wind conditions, can be heard up to 10km away, high in the Wilder Kaiser.

Tuning and playing the organ are no mean feats. Owing to its position, it experiences extremes of temperature that are an enormous drawback when it comes to tuning. The keyboard, connected to the organ electronically, is situated in the courtyard 100 metres from the instrument, giving the organist a noticeable delay between playing and hearing each note. To make matters even more difficult, the organist is not allowed to practise on the instrument itself.

Every performance ends with the tune *Guten Kameraden* (Good Comrades), a melody that best expresses the significance of this place of remembrance.

SECTION 2
BRANDENBERGER ALPEN AND ROFANGEBIRGE

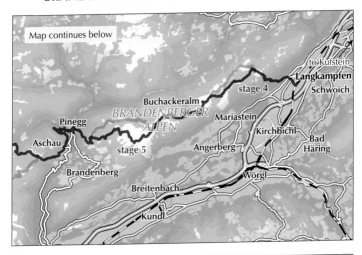

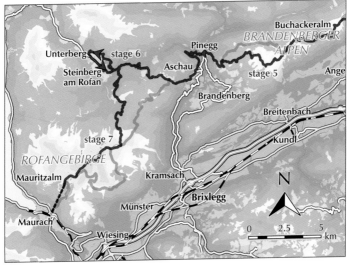

STAGE 4
Langkampfen to Buchackeralm

Start	Langkampfen station (489m)
Finish	Buchackeralm (1324m)
Distance	11km
Ascent	1370m
Descent	540m
Grade	Red (black along the ridge from Köglhörndl to Hundsalmjoch)
Time	5hr 30min (4hr 15min avoiding ridge)
Highest point	Köglhörndl (1645m)
Maps	ÖAV (none); FB301 and 321 (1:50,000); K8 (1:50,000)
Access	Train to Langkampfen from Kufstein and Innsbruck 1hr 15min walk to Angerberg for bus to Kufstein and Wörgl

From Langkampfen the path climbs steeply through forest to the meadows above. Another steep climb follows, through forest to the summit of Köglhörndl. The section along the ridge to Hundsalmjoch is graded difficult because of a descent into a notch that requires some scrambling. This can be avoided by using a parallel 4WD track through Köglalm.

The stage starts at Langkampfen station, 6km from Kufstein, served by hourly local trains between Kufstein and Innsbruck, which take 5min. Kufstein station is west of the river Inn, over the main bridge (5min walk from centre).

From **Langkampfen station** (489m), take the road at the SW end of the platform. Follow the railway for 200 metres and turn R into Bahnhofweg across meadows towards the village. Looking up, you will see a waterfall and a small white chapel above the village with L the summit of Köglhörndl and the ridge connecting it to Hundsalmjoch. Cross the main road by an underpass and continue into

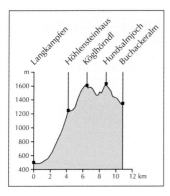

Unterlangkampfen (501m) (accommodation, meals/refreshments, shops, bank) (**15min**).

Cross the village main street and continue uphill along Windschnurweg (sp Höhlensteinalm), passing a signboard extolling the attractions of the mountains ahead. Bear L, and after passing the last houses, continue ascending on Forststrasse. Pass a forestry track R, and soon after turn R to follow a path, well waymarked by paint flashes on trees, up through the forest (**15min**).

This path winds steeply up for 3km always in forest, gaining 700m altitude, and crossing five forestry tracks. Shortly before the second track, a viewpoint looks out over the Inn valley (**30min**).

At the fourth track, the path ahead is not immediately obvious. Turn L and follow the track for 25 metres to reach a sign where the path turns R uphill. Between the fourth and fifth tracks, you pass a strangely carved tree stump containing a spring (**20min**).

After the fifth track, a wooden handrail aids a short scramble over exposed rocks and tree roots. Shortly before the top, a path comes in L from Niederbreitenbach, after which the trees begin thinning. Continue up through a stile into meadows (**35min**).

Ascend a small grassy ridge, passing a path from Jochalm R, and drop down into the bowl of Höhlensteinalm, a large meadow formed from a dried-up lake bed. The path soon reaches **Höhlensteinhaus** (1233m) (meals/refreshments, late Apr–late Oct, 08:00–18:00) (**10min**).

The tree-covered cliffs overlooking Höhlensteinalm are the flanks of Köglhörndl, and the Adlerweg makes its way up the R flank. From the rear of the refuge, pass the turkey pens L and bear L towards trees. At the far side of the meadow, turn sharply R (sp Köglhörndl) on a path waymarked by paint flashes on rocks that ascends steeply N into the forest to reach a path junction (**10min**).

From here there are two alternative Adlerweg routes marked *wanderer* (walker) and *anspruchsvoll* (demanding). The walkers' route avoids the ridge walk between Köglhörndl and Hundsalmjoch by following a path from Höhlenstein to Köglalm and a 4WD track to Hundsalm through a pleasant pastoral valley north of the ridge.

'Walkers' route via Köglalm

Take the R path (sp Köglalm/Buchackeralm), dropping down through the woods and across a meadow to a group of barns at **Köglalm**. From here, head SW across more meadows to reach a 4WD track running up the valley, with Köglhörndl rising L. Turn L, ascending the head of the valley via a series of hairpin bends. Located 250 metres after the last hairpin, a path R (sp Eishöhle) leads across more meadows and climbs up through the woods to reach the Eishöhle cave (see box). Pass a group of chalets and barns R that make up the small settlement of **Hundsalm** then continue ahead to rejoin the main route just before Daxerkreuz (**1hr 40min**).

'Demanding' route via Köglhörndl and Hundsalmjoch

Take the L path zigzagging steeply up to a kissing gate where a red arrow points the way sharply L uphill (**15min**).

The path follows the fence L, with paint marks on rocks. After 10min, bear slightly R away from the fence, following an indistinct path with occasional paint flashes. The trees thin out and are replaced by dwarf conifers and scrub. The path emerges onto a broad ridge crossing a series of false summits before passing just below a large stainless-steel cross on top of **Köglhörndl** (1645m) with a wide

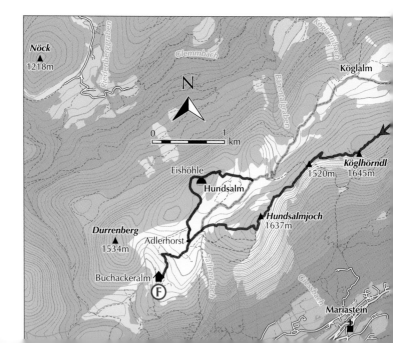

Höhlensteinhaus in a meadow at Höhlensteinalm

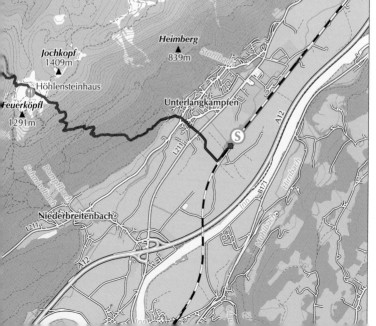

panorama of the Inn valley. Below is the pilgrimage village of Mariastein, with its church, monastery and castle (**45min**).

For the next 2km, follow the path (sp Hundsalmjoch) along the ridge, with spectacular views along sheer 800m cliffs dropping down L. There is little or no exposure. Moderate going at first, the route has a tricky cable-aided descent part way along: this section is rated black. Shortly after the summit, a path junction R gives a final opportunity to drop down to the 4WD track along the valley, avoiding the black-rated section. After 600 metres the path turns briefly away from the ridge, dropping down to avoid a big step (**25min**).

Follow a faint path R marked with occasional paint flashes and soon turn back sharply L. No signs for the L turn; ignore the path continuing ahead. After the route regains the ridge at a lower level, there is a view down a deep cleft L. Pass an old wooden cross and continue dropping down, with the summit of Hundsalmjoch rising ahead. Fixed cables aid a steep scramble into a notch, the bottom of which is the low point of the ridge (**25min**).

The ascent of Hundsalmjoch is partly aided by more fixed cables. An ancient stone wall L runs just below the cliff face, intended to prevent grazing animals from wandering over the cliffs and falling to their deaths. After a false summit, the path reaches **Hundsalmjoch** (1637m) with a modern cross (**35min**).

The Adlerhorst (Eagle's nest) at Daxerkreuz contains information and displays about the Adlerweg

Leave the cross, heading NW away from the cliff face and after 70 metres bear L to follow a waymarked path down through the forest. Cross an open meadow, then re-enter the trees. Emerge from the forest and bear L, heading downhill across meadows on a faint path heading for a 4WD track visible in the valley below. Turn L along this track to reach a peculiar-looking two-storey wooden structure at Daxerkreuz (1454m). This is the **Adlerhorst** (Eagle's nest), which contains information and displays related to the Adlerweg (**30min**). By the Adlerhorst is a turn-off R for the Hundsalm Eishöhle ice cave (20min).

HUNDSALM EISHÖHLE (ICE CAVE)

Hundsalm is a popular day-hike location, with thousands of people each year coming to visit the ice cave that sits in the forest at 1520m, about a 30min walk from Buchackeralm. A remnant of the last ice age, this is the only combined limestone drip and ice cave in the Tyrol. Inside, where the temperature never exceeds 0°C, there are limestone stalactites and stalagmites as well as permanent ice features, the most famous of which is said to resemble the head of Christ. The cave drops 40m below ground, where the snow is estimated to be 1400 years old. First discovered in 1920, the cave has been a protected national monument since 1956 and open to visitors from 1967, with entry only allowed when accompanied by a guide. To maintain a period ambience, visitors are provided with calcium carbide torches. In 1984, a previously unknown extension was opened up, and it is possible that other parts of the cave system await discovery. (Open mid May–end Sep Sat/Sun 10:00–16:00, mid July–mid Aug daily. Warm clothing recommended).

Combined route continues

Continue ahead along the 4WD track before turning sharply L at a zigzag to reach **Buchackeralm**, where you will find **Almgasthaus Buchacker** (1324m) (16 beds 16b/0d, meals/refreshments, start May–late Oct, closed Tue, overnight Mon/Tue with advance booking only, +43 699 1065 6996, **www.buchackeralm.at**) (**20min**).

STAGE 5
Buchackeralm to Pinegg

Start	Buchackeralm (1324m)
Finish	Pinegg (677m)
Distance	16.5km
Ascent	920m
Descent	1570m
Grade	Black
Time	6hr 30min
Highest point	Kienberg (1786m)
Maps	ÖAV none; FB321 (1:50,000); K8 (1:50,000)
Access	Bus from Kufstein to Angerberg, then 2hr 30min walk to Buchackeralm
	Bus from Pinegg to Kramsach

This stage through part of the Brandenberger Alpen follows a mixture of forestry roads, forest trails and mountain paths. It starts by descending into the Hasaltal valley, then climbs through forest up and over Plessenberg mountain. It continues past a series of remote farms on the Brandenberg plateau before descending to Pinegg in the Brandenberger Ache valley. There are no facilities until Pinegg.

Head S from **Buchackeralm**, following the 4WD track downhill and negotiating a series of sweeping bends for 900 metres to reach a junction (**15min**).

Turn sharply R (sp Kaiserhaus) onto another 4WD track and continue downhill through trees to emerge in meadows. The track takes two sharp zigzags before heading downhill with the **Hasaltalgraben** stream R. At the end of the meadows, continue ahead through a barrier into the forest. Turn sharply L (sp Nachbergalm) (1103m) (**25min**), crossing the stream, and follow a track ascending into the forest. After 500 metres, turn R over a stile onto a forest path waymarked with red spots, ascending steeply. Emerge into meadows and bear L uphill on a faint path to reach a gravel road on the apex of a hairpin bend. If you cannot find the path, head for a yellow waymark sign above you L. Bear R, following this road around a second hairpin to a collection of farms at **Nachberg Hochleger** (1480m) (**1hr 25min**).

Nachberg Hochleger is a spread out farming community

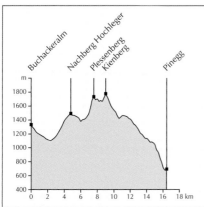

By the first farm, fork L (sp Ascherjöchl) onto a field track descending gently through meadows. This track follows the spring line and can be boggy after rain. Emerge on a gravel road on the apex of a bend and go ahead R. After a second hairpin R, turn L at a T-junction, then after 100 metres, turn L on a path through meadows and pass the roadhead R of a poor quality 4WD track (1404m) (**25min**).

Between Ascherjöchl and Einkehralm the route is graded black where it crosses the summits of Plessenberg and Kienberg. This section can be avoided by following an alternative route that passes N of the mountains following a 4WD track from just before Ascherjöchl via Aschaalm and Krumbachalm to rejoin the main route after Heubrandalm.

Alternative route

Turn R at the roadhead, then where the track bears R at a turning circle, turn L on a track that winds steeply down to **Aschaalm** farm (1326m) (**15min**).

Pass between the farm buildings and join a good quality 4WD track, which is followed for 7km. Continue downhill past a second farm R, then turn L at a T-junction. Follow the track winding through forest with first Plessenberg then Kienberg mountains rising L. Ascend gently past **Krumbachalm** farm R (1308m) (**45min**), then descend to a road junction L (1202m), where the main route is rejoined (**30min**).

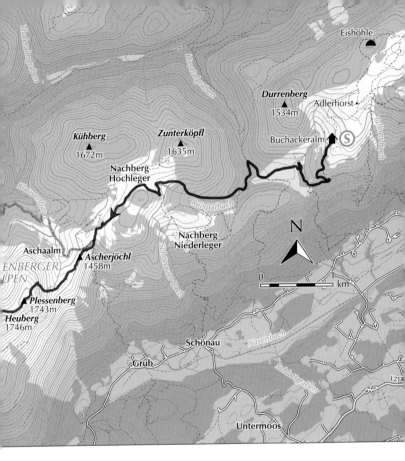

Main route over Plessenberg

Continue ahead and turn R into trees at the next turning. Turn L (sp Ascherjöchl) at a junction of paths and bear L again, ascending to reach the cross on the summit of **Ascherjöchl** (1458m) (**15min**) with Plessenberg mountain rising ahead.

The path begins to climb, gently at first through meadows, past a turning R that leads downhill to Aschaalm. Continue into forest, then follow a very steep and rocky path with cable-aided sections, eventually reaching a cross on the summit of **Plessenberg** (1743m) (**1hr**). From Plessenberg there are views all round. On a clear day Austria's highest mountains, Grossglockner and Grossvenediger, can be seen 75km away to the SE.

Plessenberg left and Kienberg, the highest points in the Brandenberger Alpen

Follow a path along the summit ridge, forking R and descending to the Heubergsattel saddle with **Heuberg** summit rising L. Turn sharply R at the next junction and ascend through pine forest to **Kienberg** summit (1786m) (**45min**).

The path now descends steeply into forest, then winds downhill to reach an isolated farm at **Einkehralm** (1446m) (**40min**). Follow a 4WD track ascending slightly through Einkehrboden forest then descending to a farm at **Heubrandalm** (1346m) (**20min**).

Bear R and fork L, then follow a track round two hairpins, firstly L then R beside a barn. Follow the 4WD track winding through woods to reach a T-junction, where the low-level alternative route rejoins (**10min**).

Combined route continues

Turn L on a gravel road and follow this downhill round three hairpin bends to reach a T-junction with an asphalt road. Turn sharply R and follow the road downhill past Arzberg farm (1079m) and continue to **Prama** farm, where the asphalt ends (**25min**).

Bear L into forest and follow a path steeply downhill to reach an asphalt road in **Pinegg** (677m) (bus to Brixlegg) where the stage ends (**20min**). Turn L and after 300 metres you will find **Gasthof Gwercherwirt**, (16 beds 16b/0d, meals/refreshments, +43 5331 5213, www.gwercherwirt.com).

STAGE 6

Pinegg to Steinberg am Rofan (Unterberg)

Start	Pinegg (677m)
Finish	Steinberg am Rofan (Unterberg) (1000m)
Distance	18km
Ascent	1170m
Descent	850m
Grade	Red
Time	5hr 30min
Highest point	Wimmerjoch (1326m)
Maps	ÖAV6 (1:25,000); FB321 (1:50,000); K027 (1:35,000)
Access	Bus from Kramsach to Aschau and Pinegg
	Bus from Steinberg to Achenkirch

This stage of the route crosses the rolling wooded hills between the Brandenberger Ache and Steinberger Ache rivers, mostly on forestry tracks or footpaths. The going is easy, although a few very steep sections make this a red stage.

From the road junction in **Pinegg** follow the main road N and bear L on a bridge over the Brandenberger Ache river. Continue over the **Steinberger Ache** river then after 75 metres turn sharply R on a path after house 60 (sp Aschau). Follow this, climbing steeply into forest, then fork R on a gravel 4WD forestry track. Continue around a hairpin bend then turn sharply L at the first junction of tracks and sharply R at the second. After 600 metres, turn sharply L on **Jägersteig** forest path, which contours through the forest, crossing a series of small wooden

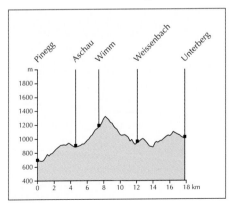

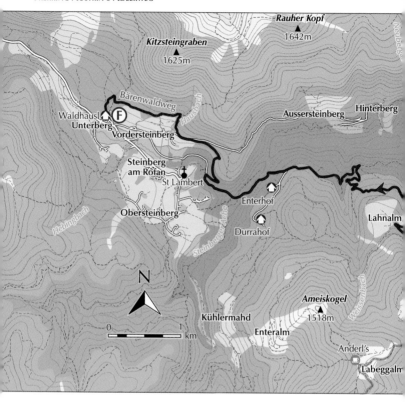

bridges, then descends slightly to reach a 4WD track and continues to the beginning of **Aschau** (874m) (Gasthof Jodlerwirt, meals/refreshments, shop, bus to Brixlegg) (**1hr 30min**).

Turn immediately R on an asphalt road, passing above the church L, and continue through the village to **Haaser** (911m) (Gasthof Haaser, 9 beds (9b/0d, meals/ refreshments, +43 5331 5512, www.gasthof-haaser.tirol) (**15min**).

Just before the Gasthof, fork R on a gravel road, then continue into forest and turn L at a T-junction of tracks. Follow this steeply up the Burgstallgraben valley, eventually crossing the Burgstaller Bach stream. Turn R at the next T-junction and after 50 metres fork L on a forest path. Go ahead over a track crossing, then bear R to follow a grassy track around meadows, keeping close to the forest edge R. Join

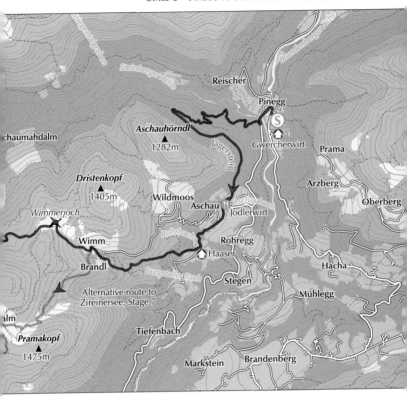

an asphalt road by Brandl farm (1143m) and keep L to reach **Wimm**, where the track turns sharply L to reach a junction (**35min**).

From Wimm farm, the waymarked Adlerweg turns N on a detour via Steinberg. This can be avoided by taking a shortcut from Wimm farm directly to Zireinersee lake (complete map and route description in Stage 7).

Turn R at the track junction over a cattle grid. After 120 metres, fork L on a forest path and follow this, climbing steeply through forest to emerge in alpine

A panorama of Rofangebirge, with Rofanspitze on the horizon and Steinberg am Rofan in valley below

meadows at **Wimmerjoch** (1335m). Wimmerjoch ridge is the highest point of the stage. Bear L to reach a track and follow this along the ridge. Where this track ends, bear half L on a grassy track and re-enter the forest at the SW corner of the meadow. Continue to reach a forestry track and turn L around a hairpin bend. After 150 metres, turn R off the track onto a path winding downhill through the forest. Follow this, curving R around a hairpin into a meadow and pass an isolated hut at **Lahnalm** (1134m) (**45min**).

Bear L around the hut and follow a grassy path N along the edge of a meadow with forest R. Continue into the forest and emerge on a forestry track. Turn L, then after 150 metres fork R on a track winding through forest. Turn R at a T-junction and descend steeply around three hairpins. After the third hairpin, continue for 250 metres then turn sharply L on a forest path descending into the Weissenbachgraben gorge. Cross the **Weissenbach** river on a footbridge and turn R (**45min**).

Follow the path uphill through forest and emerge in a meadow. Continue on a grassy path along the meadow side, with forest L, to reach a track in the far corner of the meadow. Follow this track into the forest then pass under an electricity supply line and bear L in the cleared area beneath this line. After 200 metres, follow a track bearing R into forest, descending to reach an asphalt road on the apex of a hairpin bend (**20min**). Bear L at the bend to reach after 300 metres Enterhof farm (accommodation 1 double bedroom, +43 5248 259).

Bear R and continue steeply downhill to cross the **Steinberger Ache** river (889m). Fork R, climbing at first parallel with the Mühlbach river L then crossing this river to continue on the other bank. Cross the Moosbach stream and turn R on a footbridge back across the Mühlbach and into forest. Turn L at a T-junction of tracks onto Hinterbergweg and follow this, ascending steadily to reach an asphalt road. Turn L to reach the beginning of **Vordersteinberg** (1043m) (**50min**).

Just before a cattle grid, fork R on a gravel track uphill into forest. Keep R at the first fork and L at the second across the Hausbach stream onto **Bärenwaldweg**. Bärenwaldweg is a popular footpath with extensive views S over Steinberg am Rofan to the mountains beyond. There are occasional benches and picnic tables. Follow this, winding downhill in and out of the forest, to reach Mühlegger Bach stream. Just before a ford, turn L over a footbridge then L again to rejoin the track and follow this downhill to **Unterberg** (1000m) (**30min**). (Waldhäusl inn, 10 beds 10b/0d, meals/refreshments, May–late Sep, +43 5248 206).

Steinberg am Rofan (1010m) (pop 300) (accommodation, meals/refreshments, shop, bank, bus to Achenkirch) is a small spread-out ski resort. Its position at the head of an enclosed valley has given it the soubriquet 'the most beautiful end of the world'. Inside the attractive parish church of St Lambert (passed on the next stage) are two depictions of St Vincent of Saragossa, the patron saint of lumberjacks.

STAGE 7

Steinberg am Rofan (Unterberg) to Mauritzalm

Start	Steinberg am Rofan (Unterberg) (1000m)
Finish	Mauritzalm (1834m)
Distance	18km
Ascent	1590m
Descent	760m
Grade	Red (black for ascent of Rofanspitze)
Time	7hr
Highest point	Rofanspitze (2259m)
Maps	ÖAV6 (1:25,000); FB321 (1:50,000); K027 (1:35,000)
Access	Bus from Achenkirch to Steinberg
	Cable car from Mauritzalm to Maurach

This stage takes in a crossing of the Rofan mountain range, approached via the Schauertal valley and a stiff climb to the mountain-enclosed Zireinersee lake. The ascent of Rofanspitze, aided by cables, is graded difficult. The descent to Mauritzalm over high alpine pastures, by contrast, is easy. If you want to avoid Rofan, an alternative route goes via Bayreuther Hütte.

From the Waldhäusl inn in Unterberg, follow Guffertseite SE, then go ahead at the crossroads. Pass **Steinberg am Rofan** R and continue to reach the village community centre L with **St Lambert church** behind. Turn R, then after 300 metres turn L between fields. Bear R and where road turns L into a housing development, continue ahead on a footpath (**30min**).

Follow this, winding through woods and descending to cross the Mühlbach stream. Turn R at a road junction and follow an asphalt road over the **Steinberger Ache** river (879m). After 150 metres, turn R onto a path (Steinberger Loch Steig) into woods. Follow this, winding steeply uphill to reach an asphalt road and turn R. Pass **Durrahof** farm L (limited accommodation, +43 5248 258, durrahof@aon. com), where the asphalt ends (1014m) (**30min**).

Continue ahead on a good 4WD track. Bear R at a junction, passing alongside a meadow R, then go through a barrier into the forest. Continue over a bridge and follow the main track round two hairpin bends with views R of an extensive

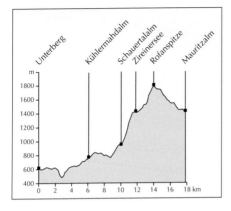

modern chalet development on the cliffs above the river S of Hintersteinberg. At the next junction, fork L, following the main track ascending steadily round more bends, and pass above **Kühlermahdalm** farm R (1139m) (**40min**).

Continue ascending, in and out of the forest, to reach a hairpin R (1226m). The track now descends gently, curving sharply round two coombs to reach a track junction (**50min**).

Bear L (sp Zireinersee) along a 4WD track that ends on reaching the **Schauertalbach** river. Continue on a path, ascending through trees and following the river. Cross the river on stepping stones, heading for obvious paint flashes on the opposite bank. Ascend a grassy ridge between two branches of the river, eventually dropping down a little to a chalet at Wimmerhütte (1350m). Cross the river by stepping stones again and ascend to a path junction at **Schauertalalm** (**35min**).

Bear R to follow a stony path zigzagging steeply up the head of the valley, gaining 500m in altitude in the next 1km. Emerge from trees into dwarf conifers and scrub, to reach the saddle at Schauertalsattel (1810m) (**1hr 10min**).

Bear L around the grassy bowl ahead, keeping above boggy ground on R. **Zireinersee** lake (1799m) soon comes into view R as you bear round to reach a path junction (**5min**). The shortcut route from Wimm farm on Stage 6 joins here.

Shortcut from Wimm farm to Zireinersee lake avoiding Steinberg

Bear L ahead at the track junction to continue past an old quarry that now serves as a car park for day visitors. The track continues to a gaggle of chalets and barns at **Eilalm** (1391m) (**55min**).

Turn sharply L and continue round a series of bends through thinning trees and pasture to reach the small **Anderl's** pasture hut (1525m) (snacks/refreshments) in **Labeggalm** (**40min**).

Leave by the 4WD track, taking the upper route R at a path fork as you leave Labeggalm. Pass a number of old goods lifts L, which once served chalets and farms in the valley below, and reach the end of the track at **Kreuzeinalm Hochleger** farm (1652m) (**35min**).

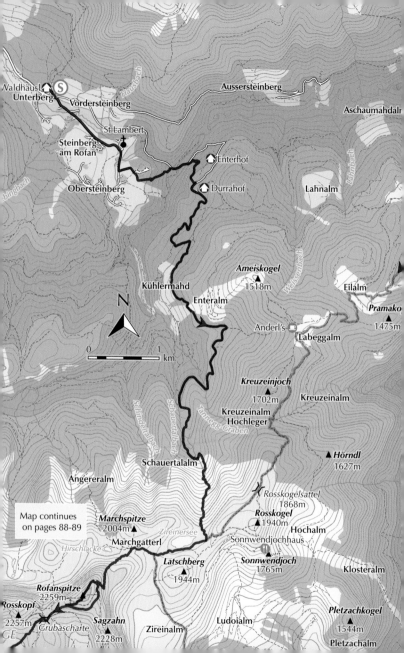

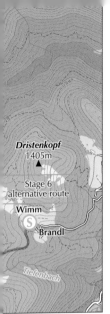

Pass round behind the barn R, taking a small grassy path that curves up the hillside behind the barn. Follow this through alpine pasture and dwarf conifers as it climbs the hillside S of the farm. Curve around the valley head, and bear SE on a heavily eroded path. You gain height rapidly, with views back across the Brandenberger Ache valley to the villages and meadows of Brandenberg opposite. When you reach the ridge, turn again to head SW, still climbing, and follow the path along a broad grassy ridge to reach Rosskogelsattel (1868m).

The path across the large grassy Rosswies plateau ahead is poorly waymarked. Continue SW, with Rosskogel (1940m) L and the steep spires of Rofan and Sagzahn straight ahead, to arrive at the crest of a ridge with **Zireinersee** lake in view below. Descend this ridge on a well-walked path to reach water meadows surrounding the lake and join Stage 7 coming up R from Steinberg am Rofan (1810m) (**1hr 20min**).

Mystical Zireinersee lake, with Rosskogel behind

WHY YOU SHOULD NOT WEAR JEWELLERY AT ZIREINERSEE

The Zireinersee is an ethereal place, which ancient legends say is filled with golden treasure. Long ago, so the story goes, there lived a beautiful fairy who, under the spell of a dragon, was condemned to live alone beside the lake. She was a kind and gentle, but lonely, fairy who craved the company of passing wanderers and huntsmen. The 'Wife of the Lake', as she was known, fascinated her visitors, who often brought her presents of gold and jewellery. However, the dragon grew jealous of her visitors and ate them after he thought they had brought enough presents. Full of sorrow that she would have no more visitors, the fairy threw all the gold and jewellery into the lake to prevent the dragon from getting it. Even today, visitors are advised not wear gold or jewellery beside Zireinersee for fear of being mugged by the dragon. Furthermore, if a visitor tries to kill the dragon, the lake will dry out and the dragon will finally be able to get hold of all the treasure in the lake.

Combined route

Turn R (sp Rofanspitze), passing L of the lake. Avoid potentially boggy ground near the shore by hugging the side of **Latschberg**, keeping about 10m above the water. The path climbs steeply away beyond the lake to a path junction, where there is a choice of routes (**25min**).

The main route climbs the east face of Rofanspitze on a cable-assisted path that can be slippery in wet weather. An alternative route circles west of the mountain via Bayreuther Hütte.

Alternative route via Bayreuther Hütte

Turn L (sp Bayreuther Hütte) shortly after Zireinersee and head S along a wide, grassy valley, keeping L to avoid a boggy area. Level at first, the path eventually begins descending with the cliffs of Rofanspitze and Sagzahn rising dramatically R. Bear gently L to pass S of Latschberg and start descending more steeply through rocky meadows with sections of limestone pavement to reach **Zireinalm** farm (1698m) (**30min**).

From Zireinalm follow a 4WD track downhill R to a hairpin bend. Just after the apex of the bend, leave the track and continue on a path R down steps, through a kissing gate and across a meadow before winding steeply downhill through trees. This path through the woods was very eroded, but path diversions and a series of steps have greatly improved conditions underfoot. A stony path continues descending gently to reach a boulder field and verdant rainforest below Vorderes Sonnwendjoch. Emerging from the trees through a squeeze stile, the route ascends gently and crosses a boggy area with sections of tree trunks as stepping stones. Bear R to reach **Bergalm** pasture hut (meals/refreshments) and **Bayreuther Hütte** (1576m) (DAV, 52 beds 24b/28d, meals/refreshments, end May–mid Oct, +43 664 342 5103, **www.bayreuther-huette.de**) (**40min**).

KARST COUNTRY

The term 'karst', from the Slovene word *kras*, is used to describe landscape where the characteristic features are caused by alkaline limestone rocks being readily dissolved by slightly acidic rainwater. The area around Zireinersee contains some of the best karst geological features found along the Adlerweg. Zireinersee is a karst lake. With no visible outlet, it drains through a series of underground sinkholes feeding springs in the surrounding valleys. The path from Zireinersee to Zireinalm first skirts a dried-up karst lake, which is kept damp by water bubbling from beneath the surface, and later crosses an area of limestone pavement, where acidic erosion has weathered an exposed limestone surface into characteristic clints (slabs) and grikes (fissures) so as to resemble paving slabs.

Leave Bayreuther Hütte on a path down steps (sp Sonnwendbühelalm), over a stile and through meadows descending SW towards trees. The path emerges onto a waymarked path contouring below Vorderes Sonnwendjoch through forest with frequent clearings. Pass over a stile in a clearing and cross a boggy area below a spring. Turn R at a path junction, ignoring the path ahead which drops down to Münster. This junction is easy to miss. Continue through a meadow dotted with boulders and cross a stream on a wooden log bridge. The path passes through a gate and ascends gently through meadows to reach **Sonnwendbühelalm** pasture hut (1645m) (snacks/refreshments, Jun–mid Oct) (**40min**).

Leave past a barn on a 4WD track (sp Rofan über Schermsteinalm). Continue contouring across open meadows, then descend steadily to reach a junction with a 4WD track coming up from the valley below (**20min**).

Bear R (sp Erfurter Hütte), ascending steadily through a natural bowl towards a col visible above. Pass a barn L and zigzag up the hillside R on a series of sweeping bends. You can see the path ahead contouring across the face of Grubalackenspitze and climbing a notch to Krahnsattel. After the last zigzag, the

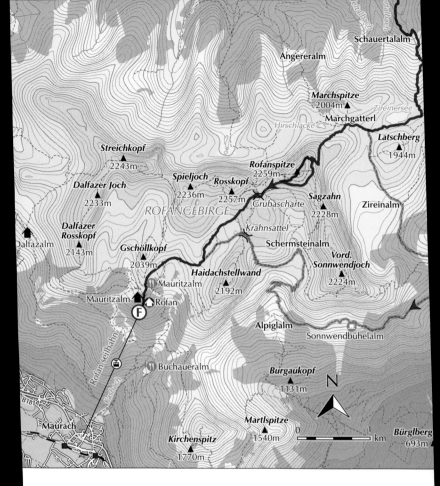

track continues ascending to join a path that has come from Bayreuther Hütte over the summit of Vorderes Sonnwendjoch to reach **Schermsteinalm** chalet (1855m) (**1hr**).

Just before the chalet, turn L off the 4WD track (sp Krahnsattel) onto a path marked with a red painted sign. Ascend a little, then contour below the face of Grubalackenspitze through rocky meadows filled with a colourful array of alpine flowers and frequent marmot burrows. Cross a number of scree tongues before bearing R to zigzag up a grassy slope ascending the notch between

Grubalackenspitze and Haidachstellwand. At **Krahnsattel** col (2002m) pass through a fence and the Gruba bowl opens up ahead. The path continues for a short distance to a junction (**40min**).

Bear L ahead (sp Erfurter Hütte), following the path down grassy slopes with the spring-fed Grubalacke lake R and the cliffs of Haidachstellwand L. A slight rise brings you to a junction where you rejoin R the main Adlerweg route (**20min**).

Main route via Rofanspitze

The main route continues ahead to a col at **Marchgatterl** (1905m) (**10min**). From here, Rofanspitze looks daunting, with the sheer cliffs and pinnacles of its N face towering above little kidney-shaped Hirschlacke lake.

Bear L (sp Rofanspitze), heading towards the gap between Rofanspitze and Rosskopf, its rocky eastern outlier. Start ascending, slowly at first, on a rocky path climbing the R side of the gap. This soon steepens, eventually reaching the top of the scree (2100m). A level section follows, contouring on a path below the uppermost cliffs, with occasional steel cables for assistance. The final steep ascent starts with a sharp turn R, where a series of cable-aided sections take you up 90m to the ridge (**45min**). The steep ascent can be very slippery when wet.

At the top, contrasting views open out. Behind, a landscape of rocks and cliffs; ahead, a wide grassy bowl ringed by the gentle rear slopes of the Rofangebirge peaks; to the S, Sagzahn (2228m) and Vorderes Sonnwendjoch (2224m); to the SW, Rofanspitze (2259m); and further away W, Hochiss (2229m).

An easy detour takes you over the summit of **Rofanspitze** (2259m). Turn R along the ridge for a short distance, following it round L to take a grassy path along the cliff top to the summit. From here, Erfurter Hütte is visible in the far distance. The Adlerweg is regained further down, by following an obvious, heavily eroded path heading SW.

The AirRofan zipline descends at 80kph from Gschöllkopf to Mauritzalm

To avoid the summit, the Adlerweg turns L along the ridge, heading S to the low point at Schaftsteigsattel (2174m), where it turns R (sp Erfurter Hütte) to contour SW, then W, around the grassy lower slopes of Rofanspitze. The detour over the summit rejoins above Grubasee lake L. Continue down a broad and often eroded path through **Grubascharte** (2102m), descending into the Gruba bowl and passing between Rosskopf R and the small Grubalacke lake L, to reach a path junction where the alternative route avoiding Rofanspitze rejoins (**55min**).

Combined route continues

Bear R over a crest, descending more steeply towards Mauritzalm, with Erfurter Hütte clearly in view. Shortly before the refuge, you pass under AirRofan, a unique cableway designed for thrills rather than transportation. Its passengers are strapped four at a time, facing down, in an open frame that then hurtles along a cable between the Eagles' Nest on Gschöllkopf and Mauritzalm. As the ride descends at 80kph, the screams of the riders can be heard far up the valley. The stage ends at **Mauritzalm** (1834m) (**25min**), where you will find **Erfurter Hütte** (DAV, 74 beds 26b/58d, meals/refreshments, end May–late Oct, +43 5243 5517, **www.erfurterhuette.at**) and **Berggasthof Rofan** (private, 60 beds 20b/40d, meals/refreshments, start May–end Oct, +43 5243 5058, **www.berggasthof-rofan.com**).

SECTION 3
KARWENDELGEBIRGE

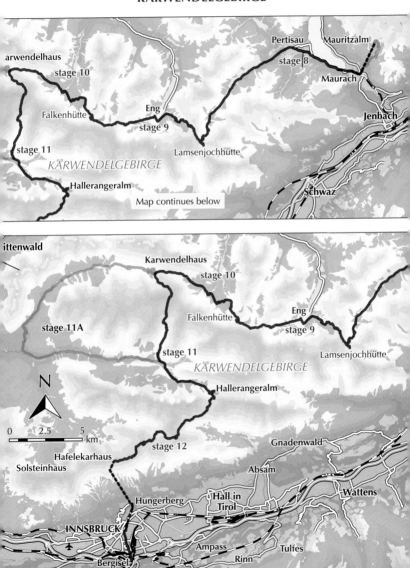

STAGE 8

Maurach to Lamsenjochhütte

Start	Maurach cable car station (980m)
Finish	Lamsenjochhütte (1953m)
Distance	17km
Ascent	1030m
Descent	60m
Grade	Red
Time	5hr (plus 1hr 40min walking descent from Mauritzalm)
Highest point	Lamsenjochhütte (1953m)
Maps	ÖAV5/3 (1:25,000); FB321 (1:50,000); K027 (1:35,000)
Access	Bus or train from Jenbach to Maurach
	Vintage bus from Pertisau to Gramaialm

This very easy walk along a valley finishes with a steep ascent. The route descends from Erfurter Hütte by the Rofan cable car (or you can walk down) and follows the lakeside path along Achensee to Pertisau. It continues on a good path through the meadows of Falzthurntal to Gramaialm before climbing steeply to Lamsenjoch.

From **Mauritzalm** the 'official' Adlerweg descends to Maurach by using the **Rofan Seilbahn** cable car from the top station between the Erfurter Hütte and the Berggasthof Rofan (start May–end Oct 08:30–17:00; mid Jun–mid Sep 08:00–17:30, journey time 5min, +43 5243 5292, www.rofanseilbahn.at). Alternatively, you can walk down through the forest.

Walking down to Maurach

The alternative walking route starts 200 metres N of the Rofan Seilbahn cable car top station, heading SE (sp Maurach, 401) between the top station of the Mauritz chairlift R and the Mauritzalm pasture hut L and following winding paths and ski runs in and out of the forest. Pass a small hut L and turn sharply L onto a 4WD track. Follow this down to **Buchaueralm** (1385m) (meals/refreshments, 10:00–17:00, closed Wed) (**50min**).

Turn sharply R beside the restaurant and bear L on a track steeply downhill into the forest. Cross another 4WD track and continue ahead, winding downhill parallel with the Kasbach stream. At a six-way crossing of tracks, go ahead R (sp Rofan Seilbahn) on a wooden bridge over the stream. Emerge from the forest beside the Alpenblick hotel and continue downhill, parallel with the Rofan cable car. Pass three car parks to reach Maurach cable-car station (**50min**).

Maurach (980m) (all services, accommodation, meals/refreshments, tourist office Achenseestrasse 63, +43 5953 000, buses to Jenbach, Pertisau, Achenkirch; train (see box) to Jenbach, Seespitz).

EUROPE'S OLDEST STEAM COG RAILWAY

It is less than 7km from Jenbach to Seespitz, yet by train it takes 45min at an average speed of only 9kph. The metre-gauge Achenseebahn railway climbs 440m from the Inn valley to Achensee with trains hauled by locomotives built in 1888 using a Riggenbach cog system to power them up

The Achenseebahn mountain railway train at Maurach

the hillside. Originally planned as a through route to Bavaria, the line never reached beyond the southern end of Achensee.

Over the years, the line has seen boom and bust conditions many times. First threatened with closure in 1927, it was saved when the power company used the line to transport materials for its hydroelectric scheme. During World War 2, it had its busiest period, transporting men and materials as an alternative route to the main line through Kufstein. In 1944, it carried nearly 142,000 passengers.

In 1955, the new road from Jenbach to Achensee opened, leading to 25 years of decline and doubt as to the line's future. Then in 1981, the communities around the lake purchased the company and a period of renaissance began. The line is now a flourishing tourist railway carrying thousands of passengers every summer from the Inn valley to connect with the lake boats at Seespitz. There is even talk of an extension to Gramaialm and on by tunnel to Engalm and Bavaria.

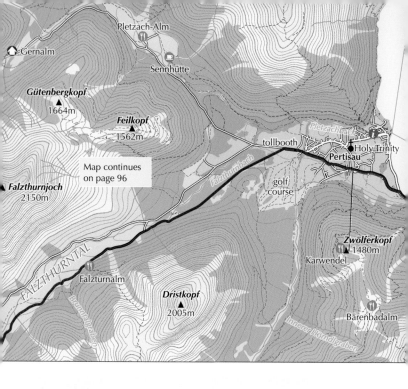

An hourly bus service operates from Maurach along the side of Achensee lake to Pertisau, where it circles the village clockwise. Alighting at Karwendeltäler, near the start of the path along Falzthurntal, you avoid a 5km flat walk.

Cross a car park in front of **Maurach** cable car station, turning L at the road and R to cross the road using an underpass. Continue ahead, passing a modern church with a grass-roofed parish hall R, to reach the main road. Turn R past a school and local council offices. Cross the road before a roundabout with a central fountain, and keeping some ornamental arches R, descend a ramp to cross the Achenseebahn railway. Turn R onto a surfaced path and descend gently alongside the railway line. After 400 metres cross the line and main road at a level crossing. Continue for 1km to reach Achensee lake at **Seespitz** station and landing stage, from where regular boats sail the length of Achensee lake (930m) (**25min**).

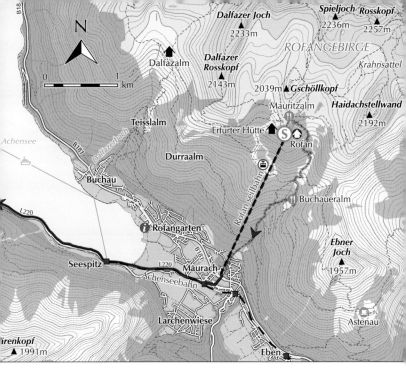

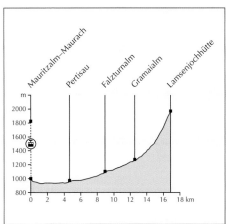

Continue along the lakeside path towards Pertisau. Pass a small green platform on the lake marking the pipes taking water 5km through the mountains to feed the hydroelectric power station in Jenbach (see box). As you enter Pertisau, turn L (sp Gramaialm), following the road ascending gently away from the lake (**30min**).

Keep straight ahead, ignoring various roads

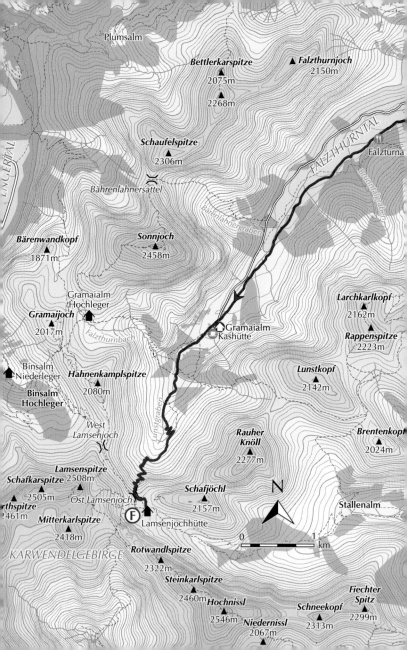

and paths R that lead into the village centre. Pass the Karwendel-Bergbahn cable car L, and bear slightly R along Karwendeltäler to the end of the village (**20min**).

Pertisau (952m) (tourist office, Karwendelstrasse 10, +43 595 30060 **www. achensee.com/tirol/pertisau**, all services, wide choice of hotels and guest houses, buses to Maurach, boat to Seespitz (Maurach) and Scholastica (Achenkirch); during peak season, a vintage bus service runs along Falzthurntal to Gramaialm).

THE RIVER THAT CHANGED DIRECTION AND THEN BACK AGAIN

Before the last ice age, the river through the valley that now holds the Achensee flowed north to south, running into the Inn valley at Jenbach. The glaciers changed all that, with the Inn Glacier, as it retreated, leaving a huge lateral moraine, while the side glacier down Kasbachtal left a terminal moraine between Maurach and Eben. This blocked the river from reaching Jenbach, and Achensee lake rose behind the moraine. The waters of the lake, prevented from flowing south, forced an exit north down Achental and into Bavaria. The river had changed direction.

This situation continued until 1928 when the Tyrolean Water Power Co built a hydroelectric power station in the Inn valley at Jenbach. In order to obtain feedstock water from Achensee, a tunnel was bored 5km through the mountains under Stanserjoch. Since that time almost all water that leaves Achensee does so by way of this tunnel, flowing south, and only a reedy trickle leaves north by the Seeache river through Achental. Man had changed the direction of the river back to its pre-ice-age orientation.

Continue ahead over a bridge and through a car park and **tollbooth** for roads to Gernalm and Gramaialm. At the end of the car park, bear L along a surfaced path leading along the broad **Falzthurntal** valley. After 2.5km of almost straight walking, at first through trees then through meadows, join a road and continue for 1km to **Alpengasthaus Falzturnalm** (1089m) (meals/refreshments, early May–late Oct closed Mon) (**45min**).

From the gasthaus, follow the track for 250 metres and bear R on a surfaced path through meadows. At a washout, the asphalt ends and becomes a 4WD track. At a three-way fork, bear R (sp Gramaialm über Wiesenweg), following the track across the river. Continuing through a gate and across a washout, the 4WD track becomes a grassy path through meadows parallel to the road. Join this road briefly then just before a gate turn L. Cross the river and join a path through a meadow on the other side to reach **Gramaialm** (1265m) with the **Alpengasthof**

The Adlerweg zigzags up the screes of Gramaier Grund to reach Lamsenjoch

Gramai (private, 26 rooms, meals/refreshments, mid May–early Nov, +43 5243 5166, **www.gramaialm.at**) and **Kashütte** pasture hut (snacks/refreshments) (**1hr**).

Leave Gramaialm by a gravel track past Franzehittn (sp Lamsenjoch). Cross the river and begin climbing, to reach a path junction R to Hochleger (**20min**). From here you can see the path ahead as it zigzags steeply to the col at the head of the valley with Lamsenspitze (2508m) soaring above. You cannot see Lamsenjochhütte, which is hidden until the last minute by a spur L.

Continue ahead as the path steepens and the gravel track soon becomes a mountain path. A series of short zigzags lead to a long traverse L to R across the mountain. Then another series of zigzags brings you to **Ost Lamsenjoch** col (**1hr 30min**).

A signpost points L to the refuge and R to Engalm (the next stage). The final approach to the refuge is confusing. Three routes, all waymarked with paint flashes, wind through the jumble of boulders that makes up the col. The shortest route is the middle one, through a narrow gap between two huge boulders, although all three converge at **Lamsenjochhütte** (1953m) (DAV, 116 beds 22b/94d, meals/refreshments, mid June–mid Oct, +43 5244 62063, **www.lamsenjochhuette.at**) (**10min**).

STAGE 9
Lamsenjochhütte to Falkenhütte

Start	Lamsenjochhütte (1953m)
Finish	Falkenhütte (1848m)
Distance	12.5km
Ascent	820m
Descent	930m
Grade	Red
Time	4hr 30min
Highest point	Lamsenjoch (1953m)
Maps	ÖAV5/3 and 5/2 (1:25,000); FB321 (1:50,000); K027 (1:35,000)
Access	Bus from Eng to Lenggries (Bavaria)

This section of the route is the first of four high-level stages taking the Adlerweg through the highest part of the Karwendel range. The path drops into Engtal valley, where Grosser Ahornboden is the home to over 2000 alpine maples (some more than 600 years old). It then climbs to traverse Laliderer Reisen below the 1000m rock wall of Laliderer Wände, the highest perpendicular rock wall in the Eastern Alps.

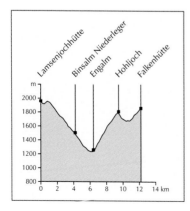

From **Lamsenjochhütte** return to the path junction on the col and follow the path ahead (sp Engalm) to reach **West Lamsenjoch** col (1940m). Here a view opens out of the north side of Karwendelgebirge, all the way to Birkkarspitze on the horizon (**25min**).

Cross a stile and descend to join a 4WD track that zigzags down. Leave the track at the fourth bend on a path L, to shortcut the next two bends. Pass a path junction R and recross the 4WD track, continuing on the path to

99

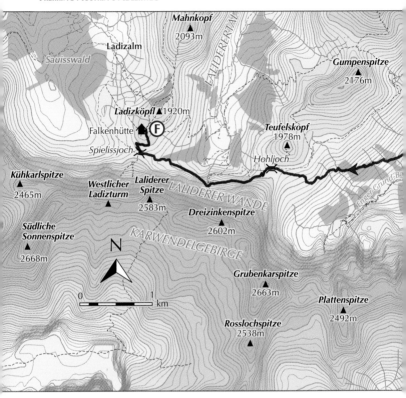

avoid Binsalm Hochleger farm away L. Rejoin the 4WD track, cutting some of the zigzags, to arrive at **Binsalm Niederleger** refuge (1500m) (private, 80 beds 40b/40d, meals/refreshments, mid May–end Oct, +43 5245 214, **www.binsalm.at**) (**50min**).

Stay on the 4WD track downhill bearing left across the head of Engtal valley.

A path descends R across meadows to **Alpengasthof Eng** (1203m) (47 rooms plus dormitory, meals/refreshments, early May–end Oct, +43 5245 231, **www.eng.at**) and the car park at the end of the toll road from Hinterriss. A bus service links Engalm with Lenggries. This valley, although in Austria, can only be reached by road from Germany.

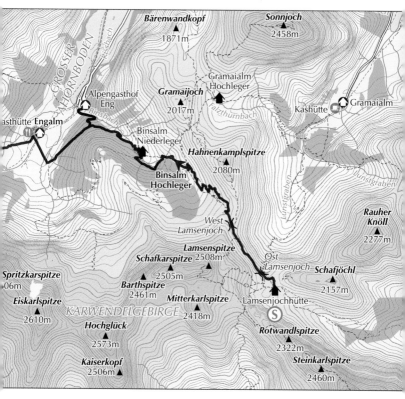

After 1000 metres turn sharply R to reach **Engalm** pasture village (1237m), the centre of an agricultural area of 510 hectares that is home to over 700 cows and attracts many German day visitors. Looking down the valley, you can see Grosser Ahornboden, famous for its ancient alpine maple trees. Accommodation is available in **Rasthütte Eng-Alm** and **Angererhütte** (30 beds 30b/0d, meals/ refreshments, early May–end Oct, +43 5245 227, www.engalm.at). In addition, three of the village farmers have converted barns to provide single, double, multibed and dormitory accommodation (**Moarhütte** +43 5245 236, **Nockhütte** +43 676 8411 8510, **Gspanhütte** +43 677 6442 5758, www.engalm.at/die-eng-alm/gaestezimmer) (**50min**).

Grosser Ahornboden in Engertal is famous for its ancient maple trees (photo: Tirol Werbung; photographer – Dominik Gigler)

ALPINE MAPLES THAT HAVE SURVIVED 600 YEARS

The valleys of Engtal and Johannestal are home to over 2200 alpine maple trees, seen at their best when ablaze with their autumn colours. The oldest of these trees have survived for over 600 years, although most date from the early 17th century. Over the years, mudflows from the mountains above have buried the trunks up to 2m deep. This has enabled secondary root systems to develop and aided the trees' hardy resistance to harsh mountain conditions. The wood is almost white, fine grained and, being very hard, has a variety of uses.

In order to protect the trees, Grosser Ahornboden (Greater Maple Land) in Engtal and Kleiner Ahornboden (Lesser Maple Land) in Johannestal have been designated Landschaftsschutzgebiet (LSG), similar to a British Site of Special Scientific Interest (SSSI), and a 10-year management scheme is in place. New saplings have been planted to replace trees that are dying of old age. A 'sponsor a tree' scheme enables supporters to pay for and visit their own tree.

Leave Engalm through a gate (sp Falkenhütte) leading to a path that climbs gently at first and then more steeply, slightly S of W, across meadows with occasional maple trees and stony outcrops, to reach the **Hohljoch** saddle (1794m) (**1hr 15min**).

Descend briefly on a 4WD track and after the first zigzag turn L on a path. This path traverses Laliderer Reisen, the scree slopes below Laliderer Wände L, the highest perpendicular rock wall in the Eastern Alps, which rises 1000m above the valley. After the traverse, a short ascent brings you to the **Spielissjoch** saddle (1773m) (**1hr**).

Turn R and follow a 4WD track up to **Falkenhütte** (1848m) (DAV, 130 beds 70b/60d, meals/refreshments, mid Jun–mid Oct, +43 5245 245, **www. falkenhuette.at**) (**10min**).

STAGE 10
Falkenhütte to Karwendelhaus

Start	Falkenhütte (1848m)
Finish	Karwendelhaus (1765m)
Distance	9km
Ascent	460m
Descent	540m
Grade	Red
Time	3hr 30min
Highest point	Falkenhütte (1848m)
Maps	ÖAV5/2 (1:25,000); FB322 (1:50,000); K26 (1:50,000)
Access	Taxi from Karwendelhaus to Scharnitz

After a gentle descent to Kleiner Ahornboden, this stage becomes a steady climb to Hochalmsattel and Karwendelhaus, with Birkkarspitze, the highest mountain in Karwendelgebirge, rising on the left.

From **Falkenhütte** follow a stony path NW (sp Karwendelhaus) downhill across meadows to join the 4WD track descending from the refuge. Follow the track R as it descends through **Ladizalm** (1573m), continuing to reach a very sharp bend R (**45min**).

Do not turn R, rather take a less used track ahead, winding downhill through the trees of Sauisswald to reach a path junction. Ignore a faint path L and bear R to follow the main path NW. After 1km, this path turns sharply L above the washout of **Karwendelgraben** coming down from the NE face of Birkkarspitze. Stay S of the river before dropping down to cross about 200 metres upstream (1384m). Continue NW into Kleiner Ahornboden and turn R over a wooden footbridge to reach the Vital Route mountain-bike trail.

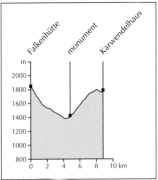

Turn L, briefly joining the cycle track, to reach a crossroads of tracks where you will find the **Hermann von Barth monument** (1399m) (**1hr 5min**).

HERMANN VON BARTH, MOUNTAINEERING PIONEER

Hermann von Barth monument in Kleiner Ahornboden

Hermann von Barth (1845–1876) was a young lawyer from Munich best known for his exploration of the Karwendelgebirge. His short but intense climbing career started in 1868 in the largely unexplored Berchtesgaden Alpen. By 1869, he had climbed 44 peaks in Allgäuer Alpen, including three previously unconquered. In summer 1870, he switched his attention to the Karwendelgebirge and climbed 88 peaks, 12 for the first time, all of them alone. The following year he moved on to the Wetterstein and was the first to climb many peaks there. In 1874, he published his book *Aus den Nördlichen Kalkalpen* (From the Northern Limestone Alps) in which he documented his experiences and tours, a work still viewed as a classic of Alpine literature. He committed suicide in 1876, deranged by fever, while on a research expedition in Angola.

His name lives on, with refuges, trails and features named after him, including Barthspitze in Karwendelgebirge. If you pause for a while at his monument in Kleiner Ahornboden, think ahead to Birkkarspitze, which he was the first to climb, alone, in 1870. You will be climbing this on the next stage!

Looking back from Grasslegerbichl over Kleiner Ahornboden, with Lamsenspitze on the horizon

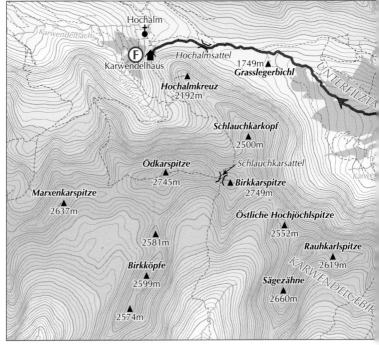

106

Go straight ahead at the cross roads (sp Karwendelhaus) along a 4WD track which soon ends and becomes a path. This climbs through the trees, gently at first but becoming steeper as it ascends the meadows along the broad floor of Unterfilztal valley. At **Grasslegerbichl**, join a track coming from the R and continue ahead a short distance to rejoin the Vital Route mountain-bike trail (1749m) (**1hr 10min**).

Follow this easily up to **Hochalmsattel** (1803m), where there is a small cross R (Jochkreuz). Continue over the col, descending slightly to a junction R with the 4WD track coming up from Scharnitz via Karwendeltal. Follow the track curving L, to reach **Karwendelhaus** (1765m) (DAV, 183 beds 42b/141d, meals/refreshments, mid Jun–mid Oct, +43 720 983 554, **www.karwendelhaus.com**) (**30min**).

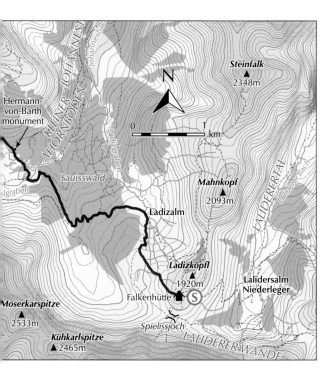

STAGE 11
Karwendelhaus to Hallerangeralm (via Birkkarspitze)

Start	Karwendelhaus (1765m)
Finish	Hallerangeralm (1768m)
Distance	14km
Ascent	1440m
Descent	1440m
Grade	Black
Time	8hr
Highest point	Birkkarspitze (2749m)
Maps	ÖAV5/2 (1:25,000); FB322 (1:50,000); K036 (1:35,000)
Access	Taxi from Karwendelhaus to Scharnitz
	Taxi from Scharnitz to Kastenalm

This is the most challenging stage of the whole walk, with cable-aided sections, some scrambling, seasonal snowfields and loose scree. It is also one of the most scenic. A steep 900m ascent, straight from the start, takes the path to a col just below Birkkarspitze, from where there is a short detour to the summit. This is followed by a long descent into the Birkkarklamm gorge to reach the pastoral Hinterautal valley. A final easier ascent brings the path to Hallerangeralm.

This stage should not be attempted in bad weather. Birkkarspitze can be avoided by walking from Karwendelhaus following a 4WD gravel road down the Karwendeltal valley almost to Scharnitz, then up the Hinterautal valley on another gravel road to Kastenalm on the south side of Birkkarspitze. This walk is described in Stage 11A. Alternatively, you could do this journey by taxi (weekdays only, Taxi Mair 05213 5363).

Karwendelbach

Hochalm
Hochalmsattel

Stage 11A

Karwendelhaus

Schlauchkarbach

Ⓢ

Hochalmkreuz
2192m

▲ **Grasslegerbichl**
1749m

UNTERFELZTAL

Hermann-
von-Barth
monument

▲ **Schlauchkarkopf**
2500m

Karwendelgraben

Ödkarspitze
2745m

Birkkarspitze
2749m

Schlauchkarsattel

Marxenkarspitze
2637m

▲ 2581m

▲ **Östliche Hochjöchlspitze**
2552m

Rauhkarlspitze
2619m

KARWENDELGEBIRGE

▲ **Moserkarspit.**
2533m

Birkköpfe
2599m

Sägezähne
2660m

▲ 2574m

**Grosser
Heissenkopf**
2437m

N

0   1
km

BIRKKARKLAMM

Birkkarbach

**Kleiner
Heissenkopf**
▲

HINTERAUTAL

Lafatscherbach

Moserkarbach

ROSSLOCH

Stage 11A

Jagbach

Kastenalm
• old mine

Reps
2160m

**Map continues
on page 111**

Gumpenkopf
1960m ▲

**Lafatscher
Niederleger**

Lafatscher
Hochleger

Hallerangerbach

The path starts ascending steeply immediately outside Karwendelhaus. Turn R (sp Birkkarspitze) and climb the steep path winding up through steel avalanche barriers above the refuge. You gain 30m height, aided by steel cables, before coming out on a path across the hillside through dwarf conifers. The summit of Birkkarspitze, topped by a cross, comes into view ahead and remains in view for almost the whole way up. Ascending steadily, the path crosses some scree tongues before passing two path junctions, the first turning L to Hochalmkreuz, the second R to Ödkarspitze (**40min**).

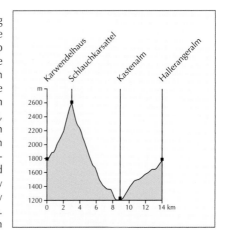

Zigzagging up the screes and boulder fields of Schlauchkar, marked by paint flashes and occasional cairns, the path crosses a depression where snow may lie all summer. A long steep crossing of scree slopes leads to another series of zigzags scrambling up the rocky lower slopes of Birkkarspitze. More steep scree follows as the path bears R for a final rocky scramble to reach **Schlauchkarsattel**, 25 metres W of Birkkarhütte (2640m), where there is an emergency shelter on the ridge between Birkkarspitze and Ödkarspitze. (**2hr**).

The final ascent to Schlauchkarsattel

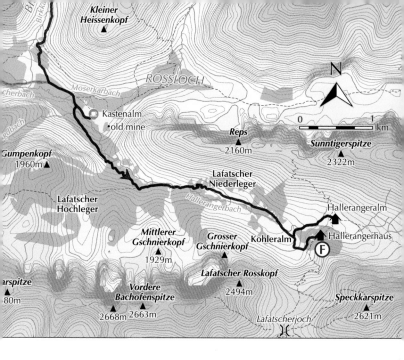

From here, a detour can be made to the summit of **Birkkarspitze** (2749m), the highest point on the Adlerweg. Turn L along the col and scramble up the first (and most difficult) part of the climb. The path zigzags up a few ledges, aided by fixed chains, passing through a notch with sheer drops either side. More chains take the path over two steps before it crosses a sloping terrace to reach the summit cross. The views in all directions are extensive. Zugspitze is seen in the west, and the Bavarian lakes to the north. To the south, the Nordkette range blocks views of the Inn valley, but the high Alps are visible on the horizon beyond (**35min** round trip).

The rocky bowl south of the col is an almost perfect example of a glacial cirque. The descent starts down a notch at the west end of the col, marked by a paint flash on rocks (sp Hallerangerhaus). Descend steeply over glaciated rocks, aided by steel cables, to reach the scree 150m below. Cross the scree following paint flashes into the bowl of the cirque, where snow may lie all summer, heading S. Continue descending, through a notch in the rim of the cirque, zigzagging down a mixture of scree and steep grassy slopes below. Eventually the path crosses to the R of the valley, reaching the treeline where dwarf conifers begin (1900m) (**1hr 30min**).

The path turns L and descends steeply to cross the Birkkarbach stream in the bottom of Birkkarklamm gorge, with more areas where snow may lie all year, some of which are crossed by the path. A long steady descent along the L of the gorge eventually brings the path over the remains of a moraine into Hinterautal valley (**1hr 45min**).

The valley floor, in complete contrast, is flat with large beaches of glacial pebbles and fluor, which has partly buried the trees. Turn L (sp Hallerangerhaus) across the beach to reach a 4WD road. Stage 11A, the alternative route avoiding Birkkarspitze rejoins here. Follow this L to reach the main entrance to **Kastenalm** (1220m) (**10min**).

A short detour takes you to **Kastenalm** pasture hut. Ahead is a private road that cannot be used to reach the hut. Instead, bear R, coming shortly to the pedestrian entrance on your L. From here, a path leads through a stile and anticlockwise around meadows to the hut (meals/refreshments, start Jun–end Sep), with the large spoil tip from a disused lead and zinc mine dominating the view (**10min**).

Turn R, or L if coming back from the pasture hut, (sp Hallerangerhaus) to cross a bridge and follow a 4WD track steeply up through the trees following the valley of the **Lafatscherbach** brook. Pass a pretty waterfall R and continue to a path junction (1490m) (**45min**).

Turn L along a level track, past the faint remains of a disused mine L. Emerge from the trees into a series of pastoral meadows at **Lafatscher Niederleger** (1577m), where Hallerangerhaus comes into view on the ridge ahead. At **Kohleralm** (1680m) the track forks (**55min**).

Turn L for Gasthof Hallerangeralm or R for Hallerangerhaus (1768m). **Gasthof Hallerangeralm** (private, 60 beds 20b/40d, meals/refreshments, early Jun–mid Oct, +43 664 1055 955, **www.halleranger-alm.at**). **Hallerangerhaus** (DAV, 84 beds 18b/66d, meals/refreshments, early Jun–mid Oct, +43 664 893 7583, **www. hallerangerhaus.at**) (**15min**).

STAGE 11A
Karwendelhaus to Hallerangeralm (via Karwendeltal)

Start	Karwendelhaus (1765m)
Finish	Hallerangeralm (1768m)
Distance	32.5km
Ascent	850m
Descent	850m
Grade	White
Time	9hr
Highest point	Hallerangeralm (1768m)
Maps	ÖAV5/1 and 5/2 (1:25,000); FB322 (1:50,000); K036 (1:35,000)
Access	Trains from Scharnitz to Innsbruck, Mittenwald and Munich

This long but easy alternative to the crossing of Birkkarspitze starts with a steep descent then follows a gently descending gravel 4WD road down the Karwendeltal valley towards Scharnitz. Another gravel road is used to ascend (even more gently) the Hinterautal valley to Kastenalm. Here Stage 11 is joined for a straightforward uphill walk to Hallerangeralm

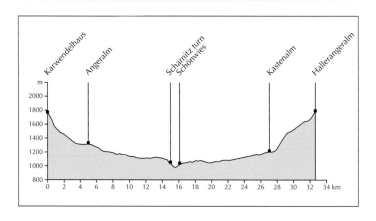

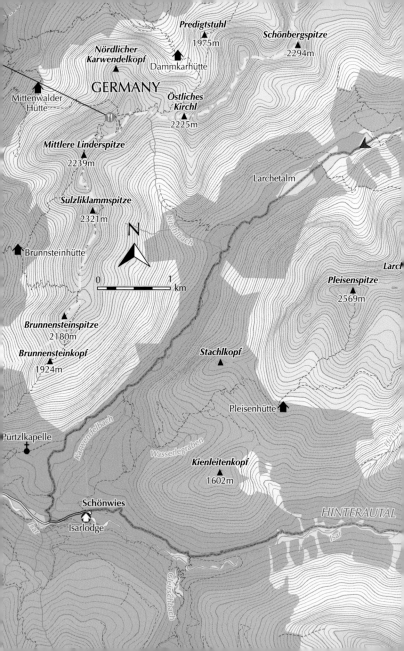

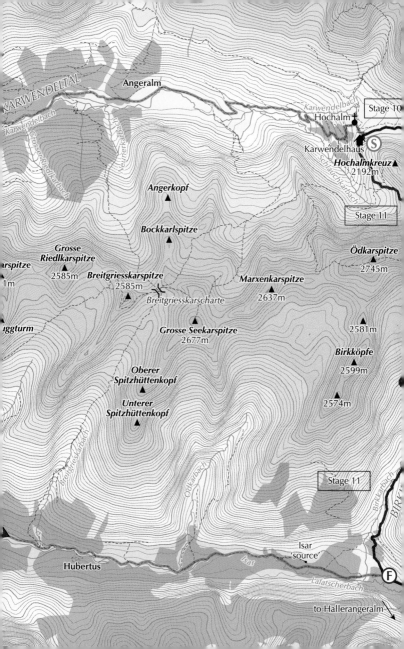

From Karwendelhaus, retrace your steps along the gravel road for a short distance, then fork L on a path that zigzags steeply down a grassy hillside. The road descends round a series of sweeping bends. The path described here cuts off the first five bends. Cross the gravel road on the apex of a bend and head towards barns and a chapel at **Hochalm** (1696m) (**10min**). Bear L just before the barns, continuing to zigzag downhill. Enter the forest and go ahead across the gravel road two more times. When you reach the road for a fourth time, turn L and follow it downhill round six more hairpins. Most of the bends can be cut off by short detours. Emerge from the forest into meadows, where the gradient eases, and pass **Angeralm** farm R (1310m) (**1hr**).

Continue gently descending Karwendeltal, crossing and recrossing the Karwendelbach stream either side of **Larchetalm** meadows. After the second bridge follow the road, now almost level, for 5km to reach a track fork. Take the L fork, still the main gravel road, and continue with views of the Karwendelbachschlucht gorge below L, then turn L on a path into the trees (**2hr 40min**). If you stay on the main track, after 2km you will reach the centre of **Scharnitz** (all services, accommodation, meals/refreshments, tourist office Hinterautalstrasse 555b, +43 5088

Karwendelhaus with Odkarspitze behind

116

Glacial fluor on the floor of Hinterautal

0540, www.seefeld.com/scharnitz, trains to Innsbruck and Munich). The path zigzags steeply down beside the gorge to reach the main track through Hinterautal. Turn L on an asphalt road and after 600 metres reach **Isarlodge Wiesenhof** (private, 20 beds 20b/0d, open all year, +43 5213 5380, www.isarlodge-wiesenhof. at) in **Schönwies** (980m) (**25min**).

After the Gasthof the asphalt surface ends and the trail becomes a good gravel road. This runs the full length of **Hinterautal**, with the river Isar R, and passes the **Isar spring** L. The Isar 'spring' is not the true source of the Isar as above the spring the river is called the Lafatscherbach, which rises in meadows at Hallerangeralm. The road continues past the foot of the Birkkarklamm gorge, where it rejoins the main route of Stage 11 and reaches **Kastenalm** pasture hut (1220m) (**2hr 50min**).

The route from Kastenalm to **Hallerangeralm** (**1hr 55min**) is described in Stage 11.

117

STAGE 12

Hallerangeralm to Hafelekarhaus

Start	Hallerangeralm (1768m)
Finish	Hafelekarhaus (2269m)
Distance	13km
Ascent	1150m
Descent	650m
Grade	Black
Time	5hr 30min
Highest point	Mannlscharte (2274m)
Maps	ÖAV5/2 (1:25,000); FB322 (1:50,000); K036 (1:35,000)
Access	Taxi from Scharnitz to Kastenalm
	Cable car from Hafelekarhaus to Hungerburg

An ascent, followed by a traverse along the Wilde Bande Steig, leads to the challenging ascent of Stempeljoch. Here an aided section (using roped planks and rubber steps) often needs renewing after winter damage. From Pfeishütte the route follows the Goetheweg, meandering from side to side of the Nordkette ridge, giving alternate views of Bavaria in Germany north, and the Inn valley south. Descent to Innsbruck is by the Nordkette cable car.

If you are staying in Gasthof Hallerangeralm, take the path that heads S across the meadows behind the Gasthof, crosses the river and ascends through the trees to Hallerangerhaus (**10min**). From **Hallerangerhaus**, take the path ascending SW (sp Pfeishütte) through trees opposite the refuge.

This soon bears L and ascends steeply up scree and loose rock. At the top, the path bears R, crossing a wooden bridge, and continues climbing, on an old mule track cut into the hillside. Continue through sparse grass, dwarf conifers and rocks and pass a cross L. The gradient eases as the path reaches the summit plateau at **Lafatscherjoch** col (2081m) (**1hr**).

Turn R following a good track that descends gently high above the Isstal valley to reach **Kohlstatt** (1978m) (**10min**). At Kohlstatt, the main track turns sharply L descending to a road head at St Magdalena, which is visible below L.

Just before the track turns sharply L, turn R and follow a path contouring along the north side of Isstal. Continue along this path, the **Wilde Bande Steig**, for 2.2km, crossing occasional scree tongues, gullies, rock outcrops and areas where snow may remain all year, with three sections aided by steel cables. A faint path can be seen ascending the bottom of the valley below the scree, and another climbing the scree slope on the opposite side. All three paths converge at the head of the valley.

As the path approaches the scree at the end of the valley, it drops down across a rocky slab to a gully where snow often remains all summer. Crossing this needs care as the area of snow differs in shape and size each year. There are

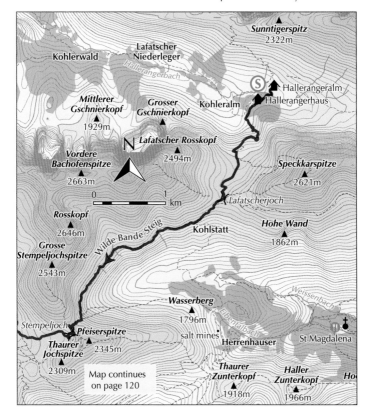

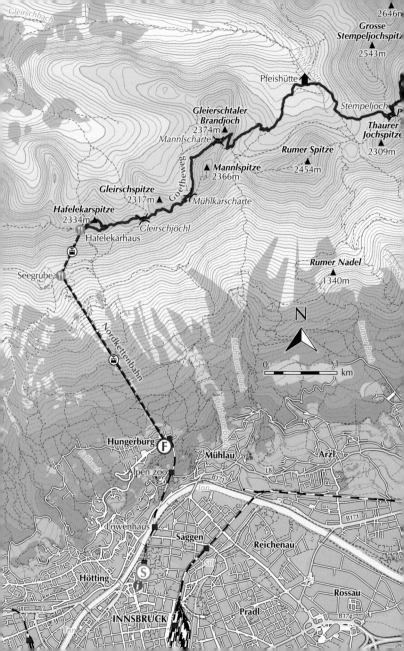

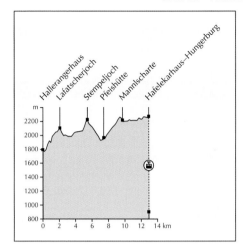

steel cables, but it may be easier to descend onto the scree and pass round the gully. By late season, this snow often erodes to form an impressive snow bridge (**1hr 20min**).

The path heads diagonally up across the scree. This whole area is unstable and a system of anchored steps and planks is used to form a path across the slope. Having crossed the slope, the path turns R (joining the path coming up the valley) and zigzags up the L of the scree. More anchored steps and planks, some of which need renewing in spring after winter damage, help you gain height quickly. After a stiff climb, you arrive at **Stempeljoch** col (2215m) (**30min**).

Descent from the col is much easier than the ascent. Drop down R on a good track that soon turns sharply back L. After 150 metres, ignore a path ahead contouring across the scree and drop down R into the bowl below the col, on a series of wide, sweeping bends. This track continues WSW across a grassy area, eventually curving round to bear NW. Pass a barn L at Pfeisalm and turn L on a 4WD track leading to **Pfeishütte** (1922m) (ÖAV, 60 beds 23b/37d, meals/refreshments, mid Jun–early Oct, +43 512 552 906, **www.pfeishuette.at**) (**30min**).

From Pfeishütte the Adlerweg follows the **Goetheweg** path, a popular day-trip excursion from the Nordkette cable car. Leaving the refuge SW (sp Hafelekar), the path climbs steadily through grass and dwarf conifers, heading for the gap between Rumer Spitze and Gleirschtaler Brandjoch. After 1km, turn R and zigzag up the grassy hillside on a good path. At the top, bear L and follow the path across the scree, turning R after 500 metres. An old path ascends the scree directly to Mannlscharte. Do not be tempted. Although the new path is longer, it is a much better option. Traverse R and back L to ascend the scree slope. At the top, the path passes through **Mannlscharte** notch (2274m) (**50min**).

Zigzag a short way down the north side of the mountain with a section of fixed cable for security. Bear L on a path contouring below Mannlspitze along a series of ledges with fixed cables. At a bend L, a painted sign indicates Zugspitze

The Goetheweg near Mannlscharte notch (photo: Tirol Werbung; photographer – Hans Herbig)

blick viewpoint where there is a good, if distant, view of Germany's highest mountain. Nearer, you can see ahead the cross and viewpoint on the summit of Hafelekar. Rising again, the path recrosses the ridge at **Mühlkarscharte**, between Mannlspitze and Gleirschspitze, bringing Innsbruck clearly into view (2243m) (**30min**).

Bearing R, the path contours below Gleirschspitze with handrails for security, after which it closely follows the Nordkette ridge, crossing frequently between the south and north of the ridge, finally passing south below Hafelekarspitze to reach **Hafelekarhaus** (2269m) (meals/refreshments, open when cable car operating) (**40min**).

> To visit **Hafelekarspitze** (2334m), turn R about 400 metres before the end and follow a short path that zigzags up to the summit, where there are extensive views in all directions. A good path from the summit zigzags down to Hafelekarhaus.

If you want to walk down to Hungerburg, it is best to leave the Goetheweg at **Gleirschjöchl**, the col between Gleirschspitze and Hafelekarspitze, and follow a waymarked path L (sp Seegrube) first to **Seegrube** (1906m) (**1hr**), where you join a 4WD track zigzagging down to **Hungerburg** (868m) (**2hr 30min**).

The Adlerweg uses the **Nordkette** cable car to reach Hungerburg, an Innsbruck suburb. This descends in two stages: Hafelekar to **Seegrube** and Seegrube to **Hungerburg** (late Apr–early Nov 08:30–17:00 subject to weather conditions, 20min journey. A combined ticket for cable car and Hungerburg–Innsbruck funicular can be bought at Hafelekarhaus).

The next stage starts at Patscherkofel, high in the mountains on the opposite side of the Inn valley, which is reached by the Patscherkofelbahn cable car from Igls. There is a direct bus from Hungerburg to Igls (route J, Mon–Fri every 10min, Sat/Sun every 15min, journey time 44min), which passes through the centre of Innsbruck. Alternatively, if you wish to visit Innsbruck en route, you can use the ultra-modern **Hungerburgbahn** funicular (Mon–Fri 07:15–19:15, Sat/Sun 08:00–19:15, every 15min), which crosses the Inn and terminates in an underground station below Innsbruck conference centre. The funicular has an intermediate stop at Alpenzoo (open daily, all year, 09:00–18:00) where you can visit the captive golden eagles. **Innsbruck** (all services, accommodation, meals/refreshments, tourist office Burggraben 3, 0900–1700, +43 512 5356 **www.innsbruck.info**, railway and bus stations, airport).

A walking route through Innsbruck and tram/bus journey to Igls for Patscherkofel are described in Stage 12A.

The Nordkette cable car descending from Seegrube to Hungerburg

SECTION 4
INNSBRUCK AND PATSCHERKOFEL

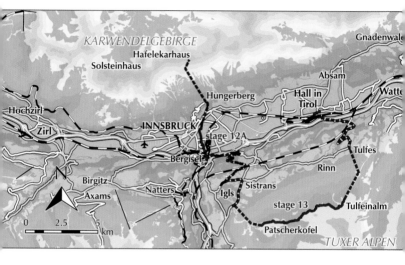

STAGE 12A
Innsbruck city tour

Start	Innsbruck, Hungerburgbahn base station (569m)
Finish	Innsbruck, Bergisel tram terminus (590m)
Distance	2.5km
Time	40min to 2hr, depending on stops
Highest point	Bergisel (635m)
Maps	ÖAV31/5 (1:50,000); FB241 (1:50,000); K036 (1:35,000)

This stage offers an opportunity to escape the mountains for a few hours and
see the main sights of Innsbruck, the Tyrolean capital. This city tour passes
places linked to three of the most significant figures in the city's history:
Emperor Maximilian, Hapsburg Empress Maria Theresa and Andreas Hofer,
local resistance leader against Napoleon.

The south side of the Triumphpforte (Triumphal Arch), which celebrates the wedding of the son of Emperor Francis Stephan

From the **Hungerburgbahn** funicular base station under the Kongresshaus (conference centre), walk S along Rennweg, with first the Hofgarten and then Landestheater on the L. Along Rennweg you will find fiacres (horse-drawn carriages) plying to take tourists on rides around the city. Pass the **Hofburg** palace R and at the end of Rennweg turn R under an arch. The building immediately ahead, before you turn, is the **Hofkirche**, entry to which is through the Volkskunst Museum L.

Continue along Hofgasse, a narrow pedestrian alley lined with tourist shops, passing the Hofburg entrance R. In the palace entrance is a branch of the famous Café Sacher, where you could stop for a piece of Sachertorte chocolate cake. The alley leads into a square in front of Maximilian's palace, which was the heart of the medieval city. The old palace is instantly identifiable by the famous **Goldenes Dachl** (golden roof) which covers a viewing balcony overlooking the square. The palace nowadays houses a museum of Maximillian's life and the headquarters of the International Alpine Convention, which promotes sustainable development in the eight nation Alpine region.

Turn L to head S along Herzog-Fredrich-Strasse, with the baroque stucco facade of Helblinghaus R. As you leave the narrow streets of the **Altstadt** (old city), you cross Burggraben/Marktgraben, with tram tracks running along the street. The tourist office is the second building L on Burggraben (**10min**).

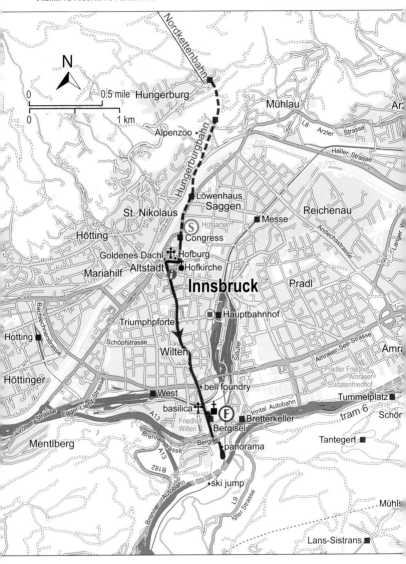

Wilten basilica is a pilgrim church on the Austrian Jakobsweg

Cross the tram tracks and continue ahead along the wide pedestrianised Maria-Theresien-Strasse. Pass the Annasäule monument (commemorating Tyrolean resistance against the Bavarians during the War of the Spanish Succession in 1703) and the Altes Landhaus L, which houses the Tyrolean regional assembly. At the end of the street stands the **Triumphpforte**, which commemorates the marriage of Leopold II to Maria Luisa.

Continue ahead into Leopoldstrasse and follow it for 800 metres as it bears first L then R to reach the **Wilten** district of the city. Pass the Grassmayr Bell Foundry and museum L. This 400-year-old foundry, which can be visited, is one of the last in Europe where bells are still cast using traditional methods. Continue over a railway bridge and pass Wilten **basilica** R, a pilgrimage church with spectacular stucco and ceiling paintings, much of which has been restored following bomb damage during World War 2. Bear L in front of Wilten **monastery** and almost immediately reach the **Bergisel tram terminus** (**30min**).

To visit **Bergisel** (635m), continue ahead past the tram terminus and take steps up to the main road. Continue ahead, then fork L on a path winding uphill past the Bierstindl cultural inn L. At Bergisel, you will find the *Tirol Panorama*, a huge picture in the round depicting the Battle of Bergisel, and the Andreas Hofer monument. A little further on is the Olympic ski jump. Retrace your steps to the tram terminus (**15min** each way).

INNSBRUCK, THE TYROLEAN CAPITAL

The history of Innsbruck is inextricably linked to three significant historical figures: a medieval emperor, a Hapsburg empress and a partisan.

During the reign of the Austrian Archduke and Holy Roman Emperor **Maximilian I** (1459–1519), the political and strategic importance of the Inn valley was first recognised and Innsbruck became the provincial capital. Maximilian favoured Innsbruck as the location for his second marriage (his first wife, Maria of Burgundy, had died) to Bianca Maria Sforza, daughter of the Duke of Milan, and to mark the occasion he had the famous Goldenes Dachl built onto the front of his palace, overlooking the main square. This covered balcony, decorated with pictures depicting him and his two wives, allowed the emperor to watch celebrations in the square without getting wet. Maximilian wished to be buried in Innsbruck and commissioned the building of the Hofkirche to hold his sumptuous mausoleum. However, this building was never to receive his body, as the burghers, enraged by large debts incurred by his court, shut the gates of the city against him. Maximilian died in Upper Austria and was buried in Weiner Neustadt.

Portrait of Emperor Maximilian in Hofburg gallery, Innsbruck

Maria Theresa (1717–1780) is often described as the most powerful woman the world has ever seen. She was the last of the pure Hapsburg rulers, and her dominions included Austria, Hungary, Croatia, Bohemia, Silesia, Mantua, Milan, Parma and the Netherlands. Despite her reign being punctuated by a series of foreign wars, she still found time to give birth to 16 children, all but 3 of whom survived infancy. Maria Theresa's main mark upon Innsbruck is the imperial Hofburg

Portrait of Empress Maria Theresa in Hofburg gallery, Innsbruck

palace, which she had rebuilt between 1754 and 1773 in Baroque style with Rococo details. She particularly favoured Innsbruck as her husband, Emperor Francis Stephan, had spent most of his early life there, and they visited the city frequently. During one of these visits in 1765, they planned to hold the wedding ceremony of their son Leopold to the daughter of the king of Spain. Unfortunately, during the festivities, the emperor died of a heart attack and the occasion became one of sadness not joy. The Triumphal Arch, in Maria-Theresien-Strasse, depicts this, with the south side showing the joy of marriage and the north the sadness of death. Following Francis's death, Maria Theresa withdrew from public life and went into a prolonged period of mourning. In later years, she claimed that her life's happiness ended in Innsbruck.

Andreas Hofer (1767–1810), a Tyrolean innkeeper, came to prominence in 1809 when he led a popular uprising against Bavarian rule. Early skirmishes saw the Tyrolese gain temporary control of Innsbruck. More fighting resulted in 20,000 rebels taking control of the city. After defeating the Austrians at the battle of Wagram, Napoleon sent 40,000 French and Bavarian troops to retake Innsbruck. At the Battle of Bergisel (13–14 August), Hofer's Tyrolean partisans inflicted one of the few defeats suffered by Napoleon's troops. For two months Hofer led the city from the Hofburg, ruling as 'Commandant of the Tirol' in the name of the Austrian Emperor. A further defeat of the Austrian army led to the isolation of the rebels, who fled to the mountains. After a final stand with diminishing forces, Hofer was defeated and forced into hiding. Captured in early 1810, he was taken to Italy, tried and on Napoleon's specific orders, executed by firing squad. In 1834, Hofer's body was returned to

Statue of Andreas Hofer at Bergisel

Innsbruck and interred in the Hofkirche in a small grave near Maximilian's massive (empty) tomb. A monument to Hofer stands at Bergisel, in front of a museum containing a panorama of his famous victory. The Tyrolean state anthem *Zu Mantua in Banden* tells the story of Hofer's tragic fate and execution.

STAGE 13
Patscherkofel to Tulfeinalm

Start	Patscherkofelbahn top station (1964m)
Finish	Tulfeinalm (2035m)
Distance	8km
Ascent	300m
Descent	230m
Grade	Red
Time	2hr 30min
Highest point	Rote Wand (2055m)
Maps	ÖAV31/5 (1:50,000); FB241 (1:50,000); K036 (1:35,000)
Access	Tram and bus from Innsbruck to Igls, then cable car to Patscherkofel
	Cable car from Tulfeinalm to Tulfes, then bus to Hall in Tirol and train to Innsbruck

The head of the eagle is a short walk along the Zirbenweg, overlooking Innsbruck from high on the slopes of Patscherkofel, south of the Inn valley. This stage provides a wonderful opportunity to look back at the mountains already visited and a chance to preview some of those to come. *Zirbe* is German for stone pine, and the Zirbenweg traverses one of the best natural pine forests in the Eastern Alps. Educational panels (in German and English) along the route provide information about the forest.

First you have to reach the start of the stage at Patscherkofel. You can take either a bus directly from the end of Stage 12 to the Patscherkofelbahn cable car *Talstation* (bottom station) (route J from Hungerburg via city centre, Mon–Fri every 10min, Sat/Sun every 15min, journey time 44min from Hungerburg, 27min from Maria-Theresien-Strasse); or a tram (route 6 from Bergisel tram terminus, hourly 10:05–18:05, journey time 17min) to reach the pretty village of **Igls**, which sits on a grassy terrace 300m above Innsbruck (all services, accommodation, meals/refreshments, tourist office Hilberstrasse 15, Mon–Fri 08:30–12:30 13:30–17:30, +43 512 5356 6080, **www.innsbruck.info**). The bus takes you all the way to the cable car

Talstation, but the tram terminates just below the village. Alight at Lanser See (the penultimate stop), then walk ahead for 300 metres on a road beside the tram tracks (Am See) to reach the main road by the Romedihof bus stop. Cross the road and take a bus (route J, Mon–Fri every 10min Sat/Sun every 15min, journey time 5min) to the cable car **Talstation**.

The two-stage **Patscherkofelbahn** cable car takes you up 956m to Patscherkofel (late May–end Oct 09:00–17:00, +43 5123 77234, www.patscherkofelbahn.at, total journey time 10min; round trip tickets available for the combined journey ascending by Patscherkofelbahn and descending by Glungezerbahn to Tulfes). Do not alight at the first stop (Mittelstation); the cabins continue to the top station. Immediately after leaving the Talstation, the cable car passes over the Olympic bobsleigh track below L.

At the top, turn L outside the cable car **Bergstation** (meals/refreshments) past **Patscherkofel Schutzhaus** (1970m) (ÖAV, 31 beds 16b/15d, meals/refreshments, mid May–early Oct, +43 512 377 196, www.schutzhaus-patscherkofel.at) where you fork R through a gateway heading NE (sp Tulfeinalm) along the **Zirbenweg** trail. For the whole walk, the view L is of Innsbruck and Hall below, with the Karwendelgebirge dominating the far side of the Inn valley. As you look ahead (down the valley), all the mountains encountered so far can be seen, with Wilder Kaiser in the distance, while behind you (up the valley)

The Innsbruck Olympic bobsleigh track above Igls is visible from the Patscherkofelbahn cable car

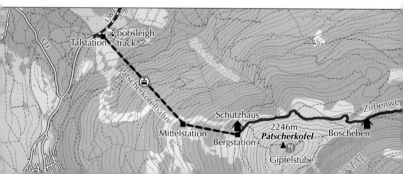

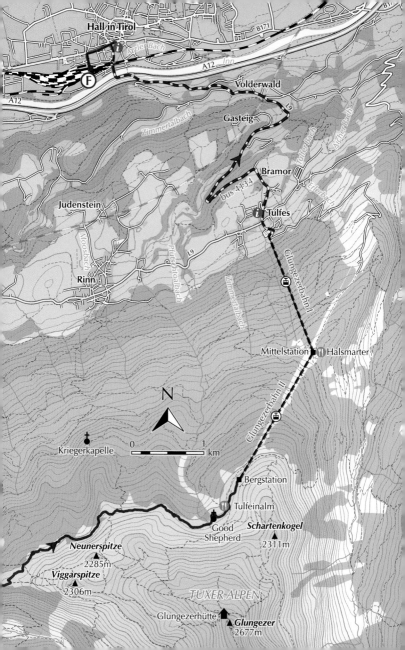

Zirbenweg with magnificent views over the Inn valley and snow-capped Zugspitze right

are the mountains to come. The path contours for 2.2km below Patscherkofel, bearing R at a path junction, and passing just below **Almgasthaus Boscheben** (2030m) (private, 19 beds 0b/19d, accommodation for groups of 5 plus only, snacks/refreshments, late May–early Oct, +43 660 234 5396, **www.boscheben.at**) (**45min**).

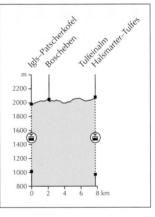

Continue heading E (sp Tulfeinalm), first south of the ridge with views down into Viggartal then passing through a notch back to the north. Ignore a turn L and continue to a second path junction (**15min**).

Turn L to continue on the Zirbenweg, bearing NE away from the ridge and pass below Viggarspitze (2306m). Winding around the flanks of the mountain with gentle undulations, the path eventually rounds a bend R (with perhaps the best view of the lower Inn valley) where the ski paraphernalia of Tulfeinalm comes into view. Rounding a coomb with a ski run below, you reach **Tulfeinalm** (2035m) (private, meals/refreshments, early Jun–end Sep, +43 5223 78468, **www.tulfeinalm.at**) (**1hr 30min**).

From Tulfeinalm, continue for 400 metres along the track (sp Bergstation), climbing slightly to reach the **Bergstation** (top station) of the two-stage **Glungezerbahn** cable car. (early Jun–end Sep, 08:30–17:00, total time 18min, +43 5223 78321, **www.glungezerbahn.at**) (**10min**). This takes you down to Tulfes via a *Mittelstation* (middle station), where there is **Alpengasthof Halsmarter** (1567m) (meals/refreshments, early Jun–end Sep, 09:00–17:00, 17:30 Sat/Sun). It is possible to walk down using a 4WD track that zigzags through the forest. Allow 3hr.

From **Tulfes** (923m) (meals/refreshments, limited accommodation, tourist office Schmalzgasse 27, Mon/Wed/Fri 09:00–12:00, +43 5223 78324, **www.hall-wattens.at**) there is a regular bus service (Route 4134, hourly) to the ancient medieval city of **Hall in Tirol** (all services, accommodation, meals/refreshments, tourist office Unterer Stadtplatz 19, +43 5223 45544, **www.hall-wattens.at**), from where you can catch a train back to Innsbruck. Alternatively, you can use the same bus route, in the opposite direction, directly from Tulfes to Innsbruck.

A DOUBLE OLYMPIC CITY

Innsbruck is one of only three cities (the others are St Moritz and Lake Placid) to have held the winter Olympic Games twice. The 1964 games were the first winter Olympics to attract over 1000 competitors. The second was in 1976, when Denver withdrew for financial reasons and Innsbruck was a late replacement. The downhill ski races were held on Patscherkofel, with the other alpine events at Axamer Lizum. The bobsleigh and toboggan run is on the slopes above Igls, while the ice stadium for the indoor events is between the railway station and the autobahn. The Austrian ski legend Franz Klammer won his only gold medal here in 1976 at the age of 22.

The most dominant element of winter sport architecture, the Bergiselschanze ski-jump hill, overlooking the city, is a replacement for the original concrete Olympic hill on the same site. The new hill, opened in 2002, was designed by the Iraqi-born, London-based architect Zaha Hadid, who was also responsible for the new Hungerburg funicular. One notable feature of the Innsbruck ski jump, which appears on television every New Year as the site of the third round of the Four Hills Tournament, is that it over-looks Innsbruck's main cemetery. A particularly chilling reminder to every competitor, as they hurtle down the slope, of the need to be careful!

SECTION 5
WETTERSTEINGEBIRGE AND MIEMINGER GEBIRGE

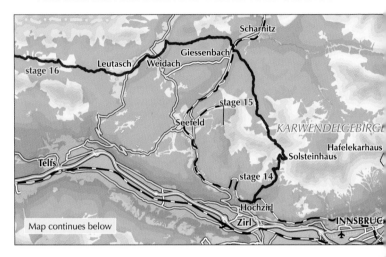

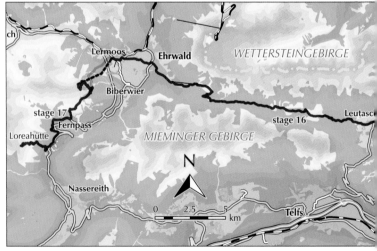

STAGE 14
Hochzirl to Solsteinhaus

Start	Hochzirl station (922m)
Finish	Solsteinhaus (1805m)
Distance	7km
Ascent	940m
Descent	60m
Grade	Red
Time	3hr
Highest point	Solsteinhaus (1805m)
Maps	ÖAV5/1 (1:25,000); FB322 (1:50,000); K026 (1:25,000)
Access	Train from Innsbruck to Hochzirl

This short stage starts at Innsbruck Hauptbahnhof station with a train journey on the Mittenwald line to Hochzirl. This is followed by a steep ascent on 4WD tracks and paths to Solsteinhaus, which can be seen on the ridge above when emerging from the forest.

To reach the start of the stage, take a Mittenwaldbahn train (destination Scharnitz, Garmisch or Munich, hourly, journey time 23min) from Innsbruck Hauptbahnhof, and alight at Hochzirl. The line climbs steadily away from Innsbruck with views over the valley. Hochzirl station is soon after the 2km Martinswand Tunnel.

At **Hochzirl** (922m), leave the station by the ramp at the E end of platform 2 (to the rear of the train) and follow a path parallel to the railway, leading into the woods. Cross a small forest track and after 500 metres turn L at a 4WD track (sp Solsteinhaus) and start ascending very steeply NE (**10min**).

Pass a house and continue ascending to reach another 4WD track. Turn R and continue up through the trees. This brings you out onto yet another wide track, which leads R around a sharp hairpin bend (**45min**).

Ignore the first steep uphill track L immediately after the bend and take the second fork L 25 metres further on (sp Solsteinhaus). Follow this track contouring through the trees below **Garbersalm**. Pass a series of small goods lifts serving hillside chalets and come out onto a 4WD track at another hairpin bend. Turn L, following this track past **Oberbach**. At Oberbach a goods lift runs up to Solsteinhaus.

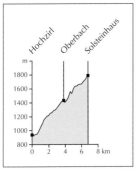

Continue along the side of a deep gorge with sheer limestone cliffs R to reach a barrier marking the end of vehicular access (**45min**).

Drop down to cross the rocky washout of a river coming down from Garberskopf, which is often dry by midsummer. The precise crossing place varies depending on winter flood damage. Head for a yellow sign on a grassy bank above the rocks on the other side, about 100 metres upstream. Turn R, bearing E, and zigzag up through the now thinning trees. At a clearing, by a stanchion for the goods lift, turn sharply L, heading N through meadows past a chalet to **Solenalm** ski hut L (1644m) (**30min**).

Both Solsteinhaus R and Erlspitze (2405m) are now in view above, with the Eppzirlerscharte notch L and the route of the next stage crossing the scree to the notch clearly visible. Continuing through the trees, the path rises to cross a side valley. It then descends slightly to cross the washouts of two rivers below **Höllkar** cirque. From here it is a straightforward ascent on a good path SE through dwarf conifers to **Solsteinhaus** (1805m) (ÖAV, 85 beds 45b/40d, meals/refreshments, late May–mid Oct, +43 664 333 6531, **www.solsteinhaus.at**) (**50min**).

The view from Solsteinhaus over a cloud-filled Inn valley to Stubaier Alpen

STAGE 15
Solsteinhaus to Leutasch (Weidach)

Start	Solsteinhaus (1805m)
Finish	Leutasch (Weidach) (1112m)
Distance	18km
Ascent	800m
Descent	1490m
Grade	Red
Time	6hr 30min
Highest point	Eppzirlerscharte (2102m)
Maps	ÖAV5/1 and 4/3 (1:25,000); FB5322 (1:50,000); K026 (1:25,000)
Access	Train from Giessenbach to Innsbruck, Mittenwald and Munich
	Bus from Weidach to Seefeld and Mittenwald

This challenging farewell to the Karwendelgebirge requires a steep ascent up scree and rock to Eppzirlerscharte notch. A long descent through meadows and the Giessenbachklamm gorge follows, to cross the railway and main road at Giessenbach. The final part brings a straightforward ascent and descent on forest tracks through the foothills of the Wettersteingebirge, ending in the sprawling resort of Leutasch.

Leave from the rear of **Solsteinhaus** by the climbing wall, and head NW across grassy slopes dotted with dwarf conifers (sp Eppzirleralm). From above the refuge, the route of the Adlerweg up to Eppzirlerscharte notch is clearly seen. Ascending gently at first, the path steepens as you reach the scree and rock beneath Erlspitze. The path climbs around the head of **Höllkar** cirque, with a short cable-aided section, and starts to zigzag up over scree. A path L leads to Nördlinger Hutte. Continue zigzagging up over rock and scree, first on R then crossing L, to reach the ridge at **Eppzirlerscharte** notch. The exact point where you cross the ridge is not obvious until the very last moment. As you climb, there are a number of amazing rock formations and spires visible on the ridge to both sides (2102m) (**1hr 20min**).

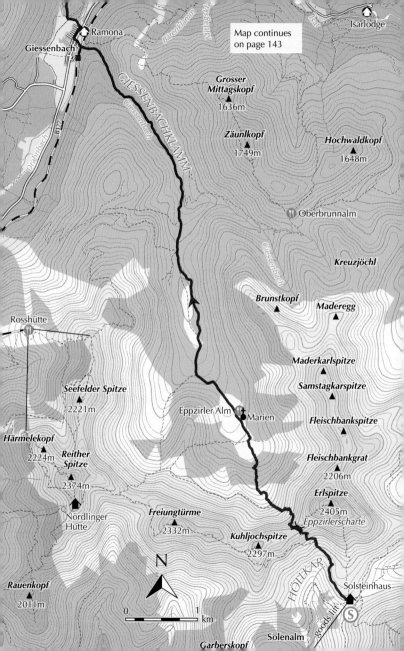

Map continues
on page 143

Isarlodge

Ramona

Giessenbach

GIESSENBACHKLAMM

Giessenbach

*Grosser
Mittagskopf*
1636m

Zäunlkopf
1749m

Hochwaldkopf
1648m

Oberbrunnalm

Kreuzjöchl

Brunstkopf

Maderegg

Rosshütte

Maderkarlspitze

Samstagkarspitze

Seefelder Spitze
2221m

Eppzirler Alm

Marien

Fleischbankspitze

Härmelekopf
2224m

*Reither
Spitze*
2374m

Fleischbankgrat
2206m

Erlspitze
2405m

Eppzirlerscharte

Nördlinger
Hütte

Freiungtürme
2332m

Kuhljochspitze
2297m

Rauenkopf
2011m

N

0   1
km

HÖLLKAR

Solsteinhaus

goods lift

(S)

Solenalm

Garberskopf

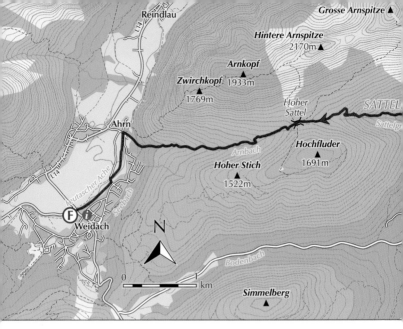

The notch is a good place to pause and admire the view. Your next target, Eppzirler Alm Gasthaus, can be seen surrounded by meadows at the head of the valley far below. The zigzag descent over scree is every bit as steep as the ascent. Part way down, before the end of the zigzags, a path L contours below Freiungtürme. Keep R, heading down into sparse grass and dwarf conifers.

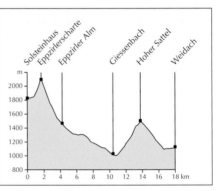

In the meadow at the bottom of the descent, cross the wide washout of a stream coming down from Erlspitze between a series of dams, and turn L onto a good track leading to **Eppzirler Alm Gasthaus** (1459m) (snacks/refreshments, mid May–mid Oct) (**1hr**).

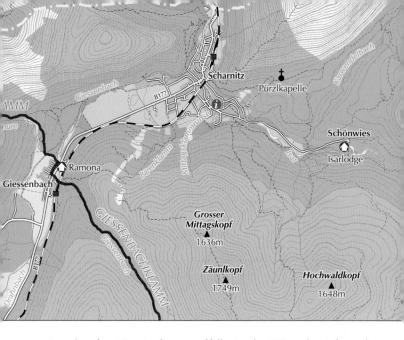

From the refuge it is a simple matter of following the 4WD track as it descends steadily for 6km, all the way down the valley to Giessenbach. The valley, broad with meadows at first, becomes steadily narrower and thickly forested as you descend. After 500 metres the track recrosses the washout and after another 750 metres it runs along an earth embankment marking the end of the washout. After passing a series of meadows below R, the track passes through a gate. At 4km from the refuge, the dirt road descends a moraine to join another 4WD track coming down a side valley R from Oberbrunnalm refuge. Continue ahead, descending steadily along the main valley which deepens to become **Giessenbachklamm**, a narrow tree and cliff-lined gorge. The track crosses the river eight times. A sharp bend L, crossing the river for the last time, brings the gorge to an end at a car park, where it emerges into the valley carrying the main road from Seefeld to Scharnitz and the railway from Innsbruck to Munich (**1hr 30min**).

Continue ahead, crossing the railway and passing a factory L, to reach the main road in **Giessenbach** (station, trains to Munich and Innsbruck). Cross the road and continue ahead. Turn R (sp Scharnitz) at the next street, parallel with the main road. At the end of this street, R, is **Gasthof Ramona** (1000m) (30 beds 30b/0d, meals/refreshments, +43 5213 5541, www.gasthof-ramona.at) (**5min**).

The Adlerweg descends to Eppzirler Alm Gasthaus (seen below), then along Giessenbachtal valley

From the car park beside the Gasthof, take the last turn L, just before the river (sp Leutasch). Fork L to reach a stream. Bear R, crossing the stream and at a complicated path junction take the 4WD track ahead heading NNW (sp Leutasch über Hoher Sattel). This track crosses an area used for dog sledge and ski/archery contests and ascends steeply with views of Scharnitz R. Sparse tree cover at first becomes thicker as the track bears L to head W into the **Sattelklamm** gorge.

After 1.5km, the 4WD track ends. Continue on a path ahead through the trees, which soon bears R, zigzagging to gain height above the valley floor. As you ascend the gorge, the limestone outcrops L become very impressive. The path continues climbing along the side of the valley for 400 metres until it reaches the start of a 4WD track leading to Leutasch. Another 400 metres of gentle ascent along this road brings you to a chalet R and the summit at **Hoher Sattel** (1495m) (**1hr 30min**).

The good 4WD track descends steadily through the woods down the Satteltal valley, dropping 400m in 3km to reach a bridge over the Leutascher Ache river at **Ahrn** (1094m) (**45min**). This is the beginning of the very spread-out year-round resort of Leutasch.

Cross the bridge and turn L on a footpath alongside the river (sp Leutasch Weidach). Recross the river at the first bridge and continue following the river to the second bridge at **Weidach** (1112m) (all services, accommodation, meals/ refreshments, tourist office Kirchplatzl 128a, +43 508 80510, bus to Seefeld), the main commercial centre of Leutasch (**20min**).

STAGE 16
Leutasch (Weidach) to Ehrwald

Start	Leutasch (Weidach) (1112m)
Finish	Ehrwald church (994m)
Distance	24km
Ascent	600m
Descent	720m
Grade	White
Time	6hr 30min
Highest point	Above Igelsee (1600m)
Maps	ÖAV4/3 and 4/2 (1:25,000); FB322 (1:50,000); K026 (1:25,000)
Access	Bus from Seefeld and Mittenwald to Weidach
	Train from Ehrwald to Garmisch and Reutte
	Bus from Ehrwald to Imst and Innsbruck

With a long gentle ascent through meadows, this stage follows the Leutascher Ache river to its source at Igelsee lake before making a steeper (but still easy) descent. The path connects two ski resorts: Leutasch, which extends for 6km along the valley, and Ehrwald, standing below the towering SW face of Germany's highest mountain Zugspitze (2962m). The trail coincides for part of its length with a very popular off-road cycle route.

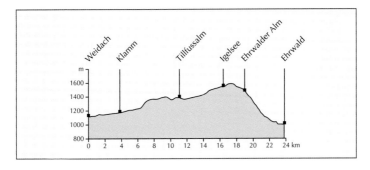

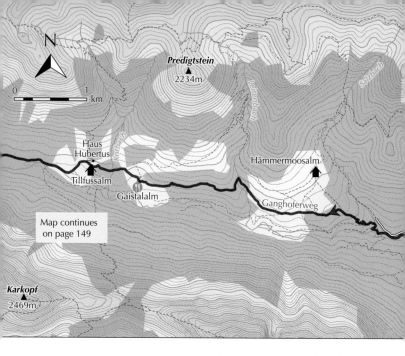

The stage starts with an easy walk through the spread-out communities that make up Leutasch. Wherever you start, head for the Leutascher Ache river and join a good track following the river upstream W. Leaving Weidach, this track can be found L of the river.

Follow the track upstream passing **Kirchplatzl** (1133m) on the opposite bank. Continue through **Aue**, and **Platzl** then pass opposite **Plaik** to reach Obern. Turn R across the river and L on the opposite bank through **Klamm** (**55min** from Weidach), where Leutasch ends.

Turn L across the river on the second bridge, opposite the tollhouse for vehicles, and follow a track upstream on the L of the river. On the opposite bank, there is a long series of car parks for day visitors to the valley ahead. After 1.5km cross the river for the last time and follow the track L, R and L again around a series of zigzags. Just before the last car park (which can be seen ahead through the trees), turn L and soon bear R (sp Gaistalalm, Tillfussalm) onto a 4WD track winding up into the woods. This is **Ganghoferweg** (**50min**).

This path climbs about 100m above the river through the trees. Fork L and emerge from the woods into an area of meadows and scattered trees, passing below **Hämmermoosalm** refuge (private/ÖAV associate, 28 beds 20b/8d, meals/

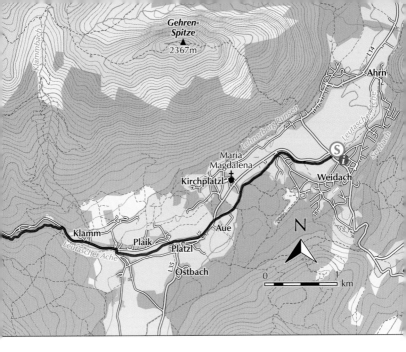

refreshments, start May–end Oct, +43 5214 51669, **www.haemmermoosalm.at**), which can be seen across the meadows R. Cross the vehicular access track for the refuge, then bear R at the next path junction (sp Gaistalalm) and ascend to cross a stream in a side valley. Continue through woods, emerging into a meadow where you will find **Gaistalalm** refuge (1366m) (meals/refreshments, mid May–Oct 09:00–18:00) (**1hr**).

Leave the refuge on a path (sp Tillfussalm) heading NW through meadows to the woods ahead. Cross a stream by a footbridge. Emerging from the woods, the path passes between Haus Hubertus, the hunting lodge and writing retreat of Ludwig Ganghofer, and **Tillfussalm** refuge (1382m) (private 9 beds 0b/9d, meals/refreshments, mid May–Oct, +43 676 610 4770, **www.tillfussalm.tirol**) (**15min**).

Pass the main entrance to the hunting lodge and follow the 4WD track downhill towards the river, to rejoin the dirt road through the valley. Turn R (sp Ehrwalder Alm) and continue ascending gently, alternating between woods and meadows. This is a popular mountain-bike route and care needs to be taken. After 1.7km, reach a fork in the tracks (**30min**). Both branches lead to Ehrwald. The R track is slightly shorter but climbs higher and is more popular with mountain bikers.

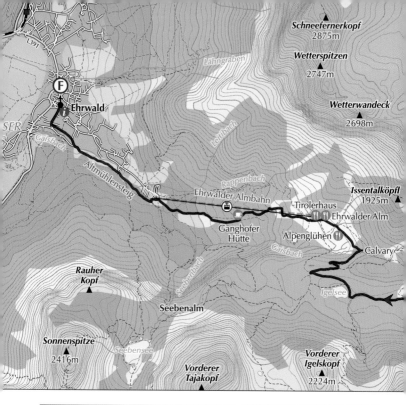

LUDWIG GANGHOFER'S HUNTING PARADISE

Although German by birth, the writer and novelist Ludwig Ganghofer set many of his novels in the area around Leutasch. Born in 1855, he originally trained to be an engineer before switching to study literature and philosophy. He spent some years in Vienna working as a playwright and journalist before coming to Tillfussalm in 1891, where he purchased Haus Hubertus, a hunting lodge. His Alpine homeland novels earned him the sobriquet of a 'world of good' writer. His works, which describe the lives of simple, competent, honest people, are nowadays thought of as kitsch, not least because most of them are set against a background of idyllic Bavarian and Tyrolean scenery.

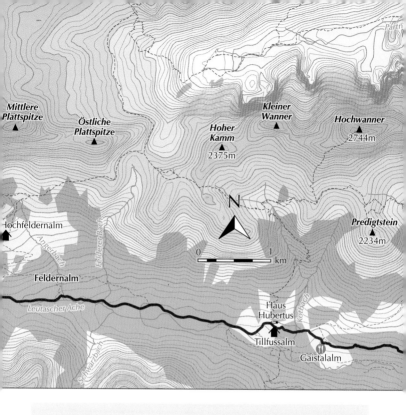

During World War 1, he worked as a war correspondent, producing reports with strong patriotic and nationalist overtones, and published anthologies of war poems. As a close friend and strong supporter of Kaiser Wilhelm II, his reports often lauded the way the war was conducted, and right until Germany's final capitulation he was still writing stirring calls to carry on fighting. He died soon after the war in 1920.

Many of Ganghofer's works, particularly his novels, are still in print, and he is estimated to have sold over 30 million copies. He is one of the most adapted German writers, 34 of his novels having been made into films for cinema or television, particularly during the Heimat film era after World War 2. His best-known novels include *Castle Hubertus*, *The Edelweiss King* and *Silence in the Forest*, which is set in Leutasch.

Near Igelsee lake there is a good view of Zugspitze (2962m), Germany's highest mountain (photo: Tirol Werbung; photographer – Dominik Gigler)

The L track is the official route of the Adlerweg. Forking L, follow the steadily narrowing river upstream, passing below a chalet at **Feldernalm**. Continue through a gate and past a chairlift bottom station to emerge into a large bowl-shaped meadow. By late summer this is often dry, but in spring and in wet weather it contains a picturesque lake, **Igelsee (1hr)**.

The track passes N of Igelsee, ascending through trees to reach a hairpin bend, with a track L to Seebensee, a popular day-walk destination from Ehrwald. Keep R, soon reaching the summit of the track (1600m), where a view of Ehrwald opens up below L, with the S face of Zugspitze (2962m) towering above. Head downhill around a series of hairpins, passing a **calvary scene** R carved into the rock face of one bend, to reach **Gasthof Alpenglühn** (meals/refreshments). After another 400 metres you come to two more restaurants, the **Ehrwalder Alm** refuge (1502m) (meals/refreshments, late May to mid Oct) and the **Tirolerhaus** (meals/refreshments, open when cable car operating) (**50min**).

At Ehrwalder Alm there is a cable car (start May–early Nov 08:30–16:30, Jul–Sep 08:00–17:30, journey time 8min), which could be used to shorten the descent to Ehrwald. However, the Adlerweg does not officially use this cable car, preferring the easy walk down through meadows and grassy ski runs.

Take the 4WD track W (sp Ehrwald nach Wiesenweg) descending the ski·run L of the cable car. This winds in and out of the trees, passing **Ganghofer Hütte** (1289m) (snacks/refreshments, late Jun–mid Oct, Fri/Sat/Sun only). The track continues down to reach a path junction just above the cable car bottom station (1108m) (**40min**).

Go ahead on a path passing the cable-car station R (sp Altmühlensteig), dropping down to the corner of the car park. Turn L through a gate and cross the stream by a bridge, then follow **Altmühlensteig** downhill, parallel with the stream. At the end of the path emerge on an asphalt road and cross back over the stream. Fork R at a road junction then turn L on a path just after house 7. Pass the tennis club and ice rink below L and Hotel Alpen Residence R to reach Florentin Wehner-Weg. Bear R and continue to Kirchplatz in the centre of **Ehrwald** (994m) (all services, accommodation, meals/refreshments, tourist office Kirchplatz 1, +43 567 320000 200, www.zugspitzearena.com) (**30min**).

Haus Hubertus, Ludwig Ganghofer's hunting lodge at Tillfussalm (photo: Tirol Werbung; photographer – Dominik Gigler) (Stage 16)

GERMANY'S HIGHEST MOUNTAIN

Part of the Wettersteingebirge, Zugspitze (2962m) is the highest mountain in Germany, but only the 53rd highest in Austria. The border between the two countries goes over the summit, where there used to be a customs post, but since Schengen this is no longer staffed. The name derives from the German *Lawinenzug* (avalanche route) of which there are many on the mountain's steep northern slopes. The first recorded ascent was in 1820 by three German surveyors led by Lt Josef Naus. However, DAV have discovered a map dated 1770 showing that local people had climbed the mountain at least 50 years earlier.

The summit can be reached by climbing or walking (allow two days for the round trip), by mountain railway from Garmisch (ascending inside the mountain) or by two different cable-car routes: one ascends from Eibsee in Germany, the other from near Ehrwald (mid May to end of October 08:40–16:40, 20min journey time). As a result, the summit is often crowded with day-trippers. **Münchner Haus** mountain refuge stands at the top, (DAV, 30 beds 0b/30d, meals/refreshments, mid May–end Sep, +49 8821 2901, **www. muenchner-haus.de**), as well as restaurants and bars associated with the railway and cable cars. The views are outstanding, with Munich 90km away visible on a clear day.

For a short period after World War 2, the US military took over the old summit hotel for exclusive use by military and civilian employees. Full board was $1 a day with ski lessons extra at 25 cents an hour. It is rather more expensive today!

STAGE 17
Ehrwald to Loreahütte

Start	Ehrwald church (994m)
Finish	Loreahütte (2022m)
Distance	19km (20km walking up to Grubigalm)
Ascent	1170m (1870m walking up to Grubigalm)
Descent	1189m (840m walking up to Grubigalm)
Grade	Red
Time	6hr 30min (8hr 15min walking up to Grubigalm)
Highest point	Grubigstein (2028m)
Maps	ÖAV4/1 (1:25,000); FB352 (1:50,000); K5 and 24 (1:50,000)
Access	Train from Garmisch and Reutte to Ehrwald and Lermoos Bus from Fernpass to Ehrwald, Nassereith and Innsbruck

In reality, this stage comprises three walks and two cable-car rides. The first walk, which crosses the flat Lermooser Moos dried-up lake bed, is followed by two cable cars that whisk you up to Grubigstein. The second walk winds over the Fernpass through forest, partly following the route of an ancient Roman road, with idyllic views of Blindsee and Fernsteinsee lakes far below. The third walk is a steep ascent that climbs above the forest to Loreahütte.

From Kirchplatz in Ehrwald, follow a winding path NW through gardens to reach a main road (Innsbrucker Strasse). Cross by a pedestrian crossing and turn R past the Grüne Baum hotel. After 50 metres turn L (Kirweg) on a road that drops down to cross the dried-up lake bed of **Lermooser Moos**. Turn R (sp Lermoos) at the first path junction on an asphalt track between meadows, with Lermoos visible ahead and Grubigstein rising behind. Continue past a golf course R and cross the main canalised drainage channel. Continue ahead to reach a main road at the edge of Lermoos.

Cross the road and turn L, continuing round a bend. Pass the Spar supermarket L to reach Unterdorf, the main commercial street of **Lermoos** (995m) (all services, accommodation, meals/refreshments, tourist office Unterdorf 15, +43 567

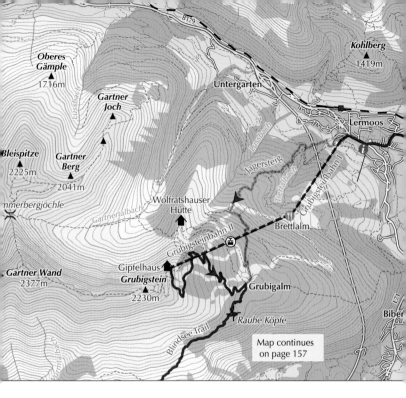

320000 300, **www.zugspitzearena.com**, trains to Garmisch and Reutte, buses to Imst). Continue past the tourist office L to the **Grubigsteinbahn** cable-car bottom station L (**45min**).

Here there is a choice of routes. The 'official' route uses a two-stage cable car to reach Grubigstein, then follows a 4WD track down to Grubigalm. If you want to walk, forest paths and a 4WD track will take you up steeply from Lermoos to Grubigalm.

Walking up to Grubigalm
Pass to the R of the cable car station and follow the road up through a series of car parks. After the last car park, go ahead up a grassy bank and follow a track bearing R. This track leads to 'Forest Thunder' a downhill mountain-bike freeride. The path

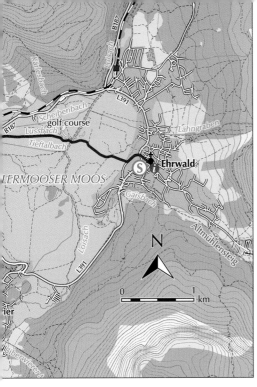

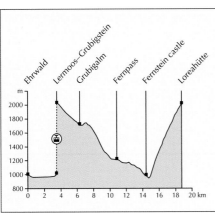

crosses it a few times. Do not try to walk up it! Where the track turns L, go ahead across a meadow then cross a small bridge and follow a path up through trees. After 50 metres emerge in a meadow and turn sharply L (sp Fernpass). You are now on **Jägersteig** forest path, which you will follow most of the way to Grubigalm. Pass under an electricity transmission line to reach a complicated junction. The Jägersteig path, Forest Thunder freeride and a 4WD forestry track all come together here for a short distance. Turn R on a 4WD forestry track, then after 40 metres turn L to continue on Jägersteig. Pass under an electricity transmission pylon and follow the path winding uphill through forest. Cross a 4WD forestry road and continue ahead uphill. Emerge on a ski run and go ahead onto a gravel road. Follow this road uphill back into the forest. After 250 metres, fork R on a forest path and follow this, zigzagging uphill, passing under the upper stage of the **Grubigsteinbahn** cable car. Emerge on another ski run and follow a broad

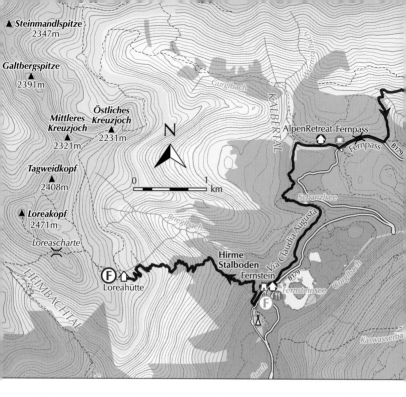

path uphill beside the run L. Turn L at a T-junction onto a gravel 4WD track and follow this uphill round a hairpin bend to reach another T-junction. Turn R, passing a reservoir R and the Grubigalmbahn chairlift top station at **Grubigalm** L (1712m). Where the 4WD track passes under another chairlift (150 metres after the top station), fork L (sp Fernpass) on a narrow path, rejoining the main route that comes down from Grubigstein (**2hr 30min**).

Ascending by cable car

Take the two-stage cable car (early May–early Nov, 08:30–16:30, total journey time 18min, +43 5673 2323) running via a middle station (1320m) to Grubigstein top station (2028m) and the **Gipfelhaus** (private 29 beds 24b/5d, meals/refreshments, late May–early Oct, +43 5673 21026, www.gipfelhaus.at). From the top station, follow a good quality 4WD access road initially winding SE downhill to **Grubigalm**. Where the 4WD track passes under a chairlift just before Grubigalm top station (1712m), turn sharply R (sp Blindsee Trail, Fernpass) on a narrow path (**40min**).

Combined route continues

Follow the Blindsee Trail winding through trees with occasional clearings, ascending gently to soon reach the summit at **Rauhe Köpfe** (1750m), and then descend, gently at first but more steeply as the trees give way to dwarf conifers. Looking down through the trees, you catch glimpses of turquoise Blindsee lake far below. High on the mountainside ahead you can see Loreahütte where this stage will end. The path zigzags down into a coomb and up the other side before turning L at a path junction and continuing down to join the main road over **Fernpass** (1216m) (**1hr 15min**).

Turn R and follow the level road for 700 metres to the **Fernpass Rasthaus** (snacks/refreshments) (**10min**). Great care is needed here as this is a busy main road without footpaths!

Turn R in front of the closed Fernpass hotel, leaving the main road, and continue on a side road past the **AlpenRetreat** guest house (B&B accommodation, vegetarian meals, Fernpass 483, +43 680 554 4324, www.alpenretreat.com). Continue through a barrier on a 4WD track descending into Kalbertal valley. At the washout of the river, turn L and follow the riverbank along a shingle beach. Fork R (sp Schloss Fernstein), then turn L downhill at a track junction. Pass **Schanzlsee** lake below L, then just after the lake fork R (**30min**).

You are now on the route of **Via Claudia Augusta**, an ancient Roman road from Verona to Augsburg. This runs downhill as a 4WD track, parallel to the main road, passing under an archway through **Schloss Fernstein** castle (980m).

Schloss Fernstein castle

WHERE ROMAN ARMIES CROSSED THE ALPS

In 15BC, General Nero Claudius Drusus, the adopted son of Roman emperor Augustus, decided to improve communications between the south and north of the Alps to support military manoeuvres in Noricum and Rhaetia (present day Austria and Bavaria). The project of converting a pack animal trail into a track capable of taking wheeled vehicles over the Alps took 60 years to accomplish, being completed by Emperor Claudius in AD47. The road was named Via Claudia Augusta, and it ran north from Ostiglia in the Italian Po valley to Augsburg, the principal Roman town of southern Germany. En route it crossed the main alpine barrier over the Reschenpass and continued over the Fernpass, between the Wettersteingebirge and Lechtal Alps. The Adlerweg follows this route for a short distance on the south side of Fernpass.

A road intended initially for military purposes soon became the main Roman trading artery between the Mediterranean and central Europe, with regular posting stations where provisions were available and fresh horses stabled. Some of these, like Bolzano, grew into sizeable Roman towns that are still important today. It was joined, in the second century AD, by a road over the Brenner Pass. The route still exists; indeed, a number of long-abandoned stages have been rediscovered, and the Via Claudia Augusta is now a popular walking and cycling route in Austria and Germany.

To reach the hotel (of which the castle is nowadays an annexe), turn L after the castle, following a track to the hotel entrance (accommodation, meals/refreshments, late May–early Oct, Fernstein 475, +43 5265 5210 **www.fernsteinsee.at**, buses to Nassereith and Ehrwald) (**25min**).

After the castle, continue on Via Claudia Augusta and cross a bridge over the Klausbach river to reach a path (sp Loreahütte) that turns off R.

The self-catering Loreahütte, on the mountainside high above Fernstein, is only manned on Fri/Sat/Sun in Jul/Aug and requires an AV key for access at other times. It is reached by a steep climb, with an even steeper descent into the Tegestal valley on the next stage. If you are not carrying food and cooking equipment or just want to avoid the steep climb and descent, you can bypass Loreahütte by taking a direct path from Fernstein to Tegestal (see Stage 18).

The small self-service Loreahütte with Loreascharte notch visible over its roof

Turn R on the track into the forest (sp Loreahütte). This ascends steeply with views through the trees back over the castle and Fernsteinsee lake. Pass Brandhütte L, continuing to zigzag up to reach a small clearing at **Hirme Stalboden** (**1hr 5min**).

As you continue ascending, the trees thin and are replaced by dwarf conifers. At 1700m, pass a memorial to old comrades L, erected by AV members of Isartal section, who operate the Loreahütte. The path soon emerges into high pastures. A path R leads to Loreaalm barns, while the main path bears L, zigzagging over a final ridge to reach **Loreahütte** (2022m) (DAV, 14 beds 0b/14d – 20 beds at weekends when second dormitory is open – self-service kitchen, Jun–end Sep, usually manned at weekends July/Aug, at other times standard AV key opens door to kitchen, common room and one dormitory, reservations required +49 8943 8944, **www.lorea-huette.de**) (**1hr 40min**).

SECTION 6
LECHTALER ALPEN

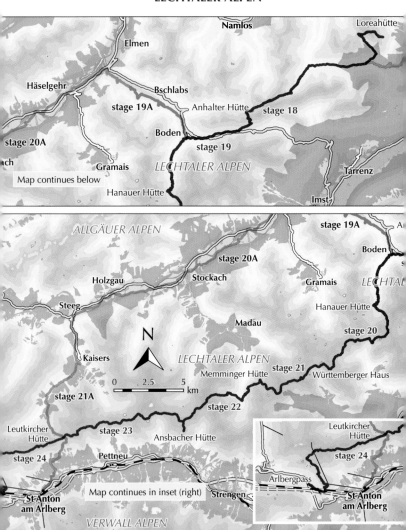

STAGE 18
Loreahütte to Anhalter Hütte

Start	Loreahütte (2022m)
Finish	Anhalter Hütte (2042m)
Distance	16km
Ascent	1260m
Descent	1240m
Grade	Red
Time	6hr 30min
Highest point	Loreascharte notch (2315m)
Maps	ÖAV4/1 and 3/4 (1:25,000); FB352 (1:50,000); K24 (1:50,000)
Access	No intermediate access

From Loreahütte, the path ascends to Loreascharte notch. It then drops into remote Haimbachtal and turns SE to reach the Tegestal valley, which is followed to Tarrentonalm. The route continues up Rotlechtal, with the sheer north face of Heiterwand dominating the view, and crosses the glacial cirque below Hinterbergjoch saddle before descending slightly to Anhalter Hütte.

Leave **Loreahütte** by a gate behind the refuge and bear L, heading W across high pastures (sp Anhalter Hütte). The path, indistinct in places, is well waymarked by paint flashes on rocks. Bear R, heading NW with rocky scree rising L. At a path junction turn L and zigzag up a scree slope with rocky outcrops to reach **Loreascharte** notch (2315m) (**50min**).

Descend W on an eroded path over grassy slopes with rocky outcrops, dropping into the bottom of **Haimbachtal** valley (2008m) (**25min**).

Turn L and begin descending on R of a stream. After a short distance cross the stream and continue on L. A faint path with occasional waymarks descends steadily, dropping over two rocky steps in the valley. Cross the stream to R for a short distance and then recross to L. The path eventually crosses the stream for the last time and turns SW towards Tegestal valley. This crossing point is not signposted. Look out for a little-used but obvious path rising above the opposite R

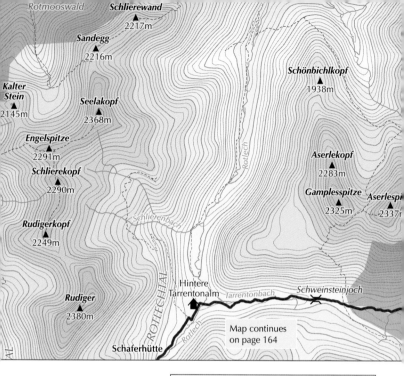

bank and cross the stream to reach this path (If you continued along Haimbachtal, you would soon start rising, heading away from the stream.) (**50min**).

Head SW on a little-used and poorly waymarked path through the forest, rising a little at first before dropping to join a 4WD track running up **Tegestal** (**30min**). The alternative route from Fernstein avoiding Loreahütte rejoins here.

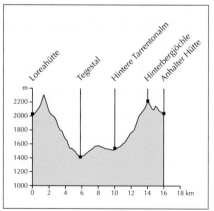

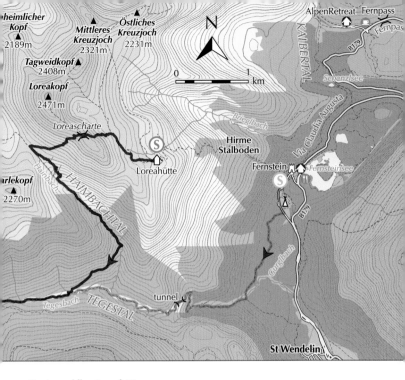

Route avoiding Loreahütte

From Stage 17 Via Claudia Augusta, continue ahead and join the surfaced road that links the hotel with the campsite. Continue past the campsite then after 100 metres turn R (sp Tarrentonalm) onto a 4WD track leading into the woods. Follow this gently undulating track, forking R (sp Nassereith) at a path junction. The track closely follows the route of an electricity supply line before emerging into Tegestal valley (935m) (**30min**).

Turn R (sp Tarrentonalm) to head W on a good 4WD track running the full length of the valley. A series of steep hairpins and a short tunnel ascend 200m up a moraine. Continue to ascend, less steeply, along a well-forested deep valley. Stage 18 from Loreahütte joins from the R immediately after a bridge over a small stream (**1hr**).

Main route

Turn R (sp Tarrentonalm) along the 4WD track, bearing R uphill at a track fork. The tree cover thins out and occasional meadows appear. Pass a ruined farm L to reach a col just beyond **Schweinsteinjoch**, beside a seasonal lake (1564m). Continue ahead, descending slightly and bear R at a track fork. Pass an abandoned zinc mine L, then turn L at a path junction to reach **Hintere Tarrentonalm** farm and pasture hut (1519m) (private, 9 beds 4b/5d, snacks/refreshments, mid Jun–mid Sep, +43 660 296 7669, steffi.erhart@gmail.com) (**1hr**).

Leave Tarrentonalm via a gate through the farmyard and head SW on a 4WD track turning sharply R after 200 metres. At the next junction turn L (sp Anhalter Hütte), following a 4WD track that leads to a chalet at **Schaferhütte** R (**15min**).

The 4WD track ends here, and a faint path continues ahead, ascending the valley. Trees give way to dwarf pines, and these in turn give way to grassy slopes with rocky outcrops and scree tongues. Waymarking is by paint flashes on rocks and free-standing metal posts. After 1.5km, the valley bears slightly R (**40min**).

At this point, the path zigzags steeply up a moraine and then continues to gain height, climbing steadily along the R side of the valley above. The formidable wall and spires of Heiterwand L dominate the view across the valley, while looking back, you can clearly see Zugspitze. The sheer face of Heiterwand is an excellent sounding board, and the noise of sheep bleating on the hillsides high above

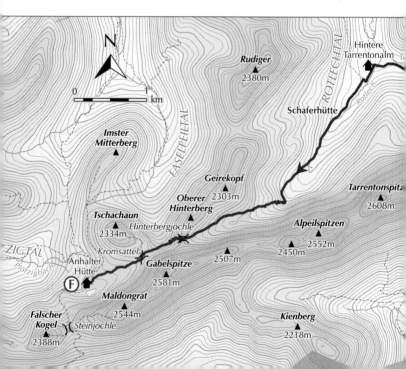

From Hinterbergjöchle, the Adlerweg drops steeply into the Faselfeiltal bowl, then climbs across screes below Gabelspitz

often echoes with a surreal tone. The path ascends across a grassy hillside with occasional rocky outcrops and scree tongues. A final path up the side of the scree brings the path to the col at **Hinterbergjöchle** (2203m) (**1hr 5min**).

This is a very impressive spot. A deep bowl ahead forms a glacial cirque at the head of Faselfeiltal valley, which drops away R, while Gabelspitze (2581m) towers above L. The next target for the Adlerweg, Kromsattel col, can be seen straight ahead on the other side of the bowl. The path crosses the wooden fence on the col by a stile and drops very steeply into the cirque ahead, so take care in selecting the correct line of descent. Do not be tempted by what looks like a route straight down. Instead, turn R (sp Anhalter Hütte) along the rim, past some large boulders, to a sign painted on rocks. Here a path zigzags into the bottom of the bowl then cuts across the scree to **Kromsattel** (2137m) (**35min**).

From the col a path leads steadily down WSW across grassy slopes to **Anhalter Hütte**, which can soon be seen ahead (2042m) (DAV, 75 beds 13b/62d, meals/refreshments, mid Jun–end Sep, +43 660 664 7428, www.anhalter-huette. de) (**20min**).

STAGE 19

Anhalter Hütte to Hanauer Hütte

Start	Anhalter Hütte (2042m)
Finish	Hanauer Hütte (1922m)
Distance	12.5km
Ascent	750m
Descent	870m
Grade	Red
Time	4hr 15min
Highest point	Steinjöchle col (2198m)
Maps	ÖAV3/4 (1:25,000); FB351 (1:50,000); K24 (1:50,000)
Access	Bus from Hahntennjoch, Pfafflar and Boden to Elmen and Imst

The route climbs steeply S over Steinjöchle col and descends to meet the road from Lechtal at Hahntennjoch. It follows this road W down Pfafflartal valley through the remote communities of Pfafflar and Boden before turning S again to ascend Angerletal to Hanauer Hütte, high above the head of the valley.

Anhalter Hütte with Maldongrat rising behind

Leave Anhalter Hütte SW (sp Hahntennjoch), dropping down a little to cross meadows with seasonal Kromsee lake L. Pass two small huts R and bear L, climbing round the corner of Maldongrat and continuing to ascend steeply across the hillside, above the screes of Falscher Kogel. A series of zigzags bring the path up the cliffs, with fixed cables for security, to reach **Steinjöchle** col (2198m) (**40min**).

Descend across tussock grass, initially SE but soon bearing S, with the road pass between Boden and Imst visible below. Continue SW through dwarf conifers, dropping down to a point just before extensive car parking alongside the road at **Hahntennjoch** (1894m) (**15min**).

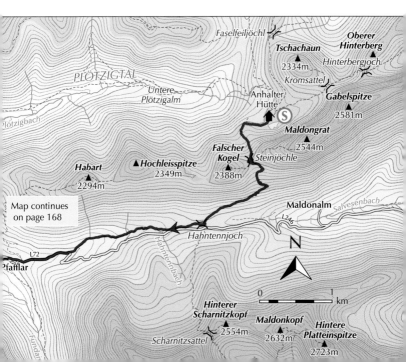

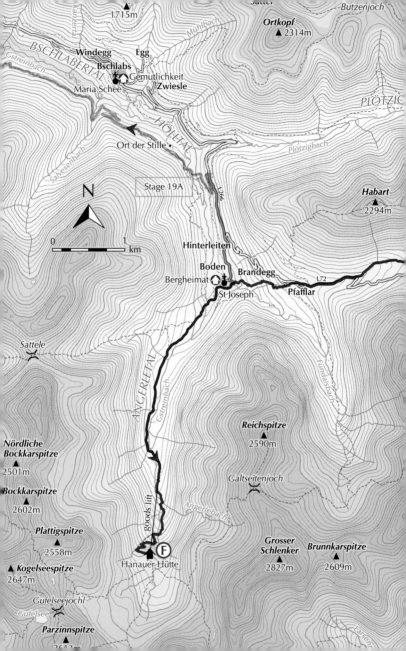

Stage 19A

Boden is a small village with a church and guest house

Turn R (sp Boden), passing through a fence, and continue on a path through meadows parallel to the road descending towards Pfafflar. This path comes out beside a stream L. Follow this for 2km before joining the road at a sharp hairpin bend. Walk along the side of the road for 600 metres to the tiny community of **Pfafflar** (1619m) (**50min**).

Continue along the road for 250 metres and turn L across the stream on a small wooden bridge. This turn is easy to miss. Bear R downhill on a narrow path through trees to reach a 4WD track and turn L. After 40 metres, turn R just before a farm entrance on a path into trees and continue winding downhill. Emerge from the trees and bear R to recross the stream below a small dam R. Continue ahead on another 4WD track for 170 metres, then turn sharply L (sp Boden) and follow a path down through meadows to the village of **Boden** (1356m) (**Gasthof Bergheimat** 40 beds, meals/refreshments, +43 5635 231) (**30min**).

The next six stages follow a high-level route through the Lectaler Alpen. While they are all walkers' routes and no climbing equipment is required, there are exposed sections where passage is aided by chains and short ladders. You need to be experienced in mountain walking and have stamina and a good head for heights to complete these stages. An alternative route

Looking up Angerletal from above Boden

from Boden through the Lechtal valley, which bypasses the Lechtaler Alpen, is described in Stages 19A–21A. If you do start the high-level route, every refuge passed has its own access route that you can use to escape to the valley if the weather deteriorates or the going gets too tough.

Turn L over the bridge just before the village and bear R (sp Angerletal) on a 4WD track. Fork R and drop downhill to cross the Angerlebach river. Turn L along a good track steadily ascending **Angerletal** for 3km. As you look ahead, Hanauer Hütte comes into view, perched above the end of the valley, with Dremelspitze (2733m) towering above. Shortly before the head of the valley, recross the river and arrive at the bottom station of the Hanauer Hütte **goods lift** L (1529m) (**1hr**).

From here, the path ascends the steepening valley through dwarf conifers and scrub, bridging two streams. Just after the second bridge, fork L and pass below the refuge. Turn R and zigzag up to reach the ridge 150 metres W of the refuge. Turn L to reach **Hanauer Hütte** (1922m) (DAV, 124 beds 22b/102d, meals/refreshments, mid Jun–early Oct, +43 664 266 9149, **www.hanauer-huette.de**) (**1hr**).

STAGE 20
Hanauer Hütte to Württemberger Haus

Start	Hanauer Hütte (1992m)
Finish	Württemberger Haus (2220m)
Distance	11km
Ascent	1300m
Descent	1000m
Grade	Black
Time	7hr
Highest point	Hintere Dremelscharte (2470m)
Maps	ÖAV3/4 and 3/3 (1:25,000); FB351 (1:50,000); K24 (1:50,000)
Access	No intermediate access

This stage of the route is spent almost entirely above 2000m and traverses three high-level cols. From Hanauer Hütte a steady ascent over scree slopes to Hintere Dremelscharte notch takes the route over the main Lechtaler Alpen ridgeline. A steep descent to tiny Steinsee lake is followed by a series of long contouring traverses on scree or tussock grass along the south side of the main ridge, rising and falling to cross two radial ridges. One of these crossings, Rosskarscharte, is the second most challenging part of the Adlerweg.

Dremelspitze can be crossed through notches either east (Hintere Dremelscharte) or west (Vordere Dremelscharte) of the summit. The Adlerweg takes the eastern Hintere Dremelscharte route.

Leave **Hanauer Hütte** on a path S and after 75 metres fork L (sp Steinseehütte). The R fork is a direct route to Württemberger Haus (5hr 30min) via Gufelseejöchl and Bitterscharte, bypassing Dremelscharte. In 100 metres you reach another fork with a choice of routes to Steinseehütte. Fork L for Hintere Dremelscharte and cross a bridge over Gstreinbach stream. The path starts ascending steeply through tussock grass and dwarf conifers and passes a turning L for Galtseitenjoch. The going becomes rockier as you gain height, with talus and scree replacing grass after 2100m altitude is reached. The gradient eases at 2250m and the route passes

The Adlerweg descends through Hintere Dremelscharte towards Steinsee (photo: Tirol Werbung; photographer – Dominik Gigler) (Stage 20)

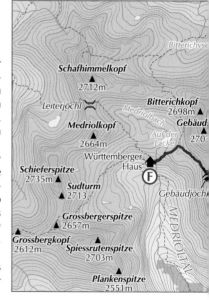

a seasonal snow-melt lake L. After 2350m the path steepens again, passing through a debris-filled gully with cable assistance as it climbs between Dremelspitze R and Hanauer Spitze L to reach **Hintere Dremelscharte** notch (2470m) (**2hr**).

From the notch, descend steeply over scree slopes to reach the shore of **Steinsee** lake, then continue gently downhill over tussock grass to **Steinseehütte** (2061m) (ÖAV, 84 beds 24b/60d, meals/refreshments, early Jun–mid Sep, +43 660 491 7124, www.steinseehuette.at) (**1hr 15min**).

From the refuge, the path drops down a little N (sp Württemberger

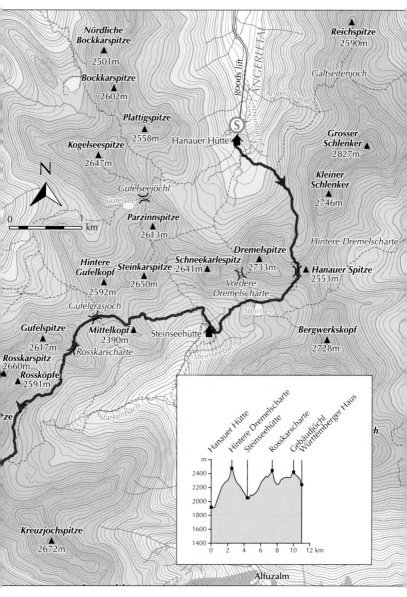

Nördliche
Bockkarspitze
▲
2501m

Bockkarspitze
▲
2602m

Plattigspitze
▲
2558m

Hanauer Hütte

Kogelseespitze
▲
2647m

goods lift

ANGERLETAL

Ostertalbach

Angerlebach

Reichspitze
▲
2590m

Galtseitenjoch

Ⓢ

Grosser
Schlenker ▲
2827m

Kleiner
Schlenker
▲
2746m

N

Gufelseejöchl
Gufelsee

0   1
└─────────┘ km

Parzinnspitze
▲
2613m

Dremelspitze
▲
2733m

Hintere Dremelscharte

Hanauer Spitze
▲ 2553m

Hintere
Gufelkopf
▲
2592m

Steinkarspitze
▲
2650m

Schneekarlespitz
2641m ▲

Vordere
Dremelscharte

Gufelgrasjoch

Steinsee

Gufelspitze
▲
2617m

Rosskarspitz
▲ 2660m
Rossköpfe
▲ 2591m

Mittelkopf
▲ 2390m
Rosskarscharte

Steinseehütte

Steinseebach

Bergwerkskopf
▲
2728m

ze

Starkenbach

Kreuzjochspitze
▲
2672m

Alfuzalm

173

Württemberger Haus is reached by a small bridge over a ravine

Haus) across grassy slopes and through dwarf conifers to cross a stream, then rises steeply to a path junction below the shoulder of Schneekarlespitz. Turn L and contour below the screes of Steinkarspitze, heading for the gap ahead between Mittelkopf and Hintere Gufelkopf. Continue ahead, ascending a grassy tongue with rocky outcrops, to reach a col (2302m) (**1hr**).

At the col turn R and ascend slightly to contour around the scree slopes of Gufelgras bowl, which can be seen ahead. Continue ahead at a path junction, passing just below **Gufelgrasjoch** col R. The bowl closes in ahead and the path continues contouring across the screes of Gufelspitze, up the R side of a wide gully. Near the head of the gully, painted signs indicate where the path turns uphill R, scrambling steeply over rocks to reach **Rosskarscharte** col (2458m) (**45min**).

Over the col, the path drops steeply 200m, first through a gully with fixed chains for assistance, then across scree, bearing L to reach sparse grass with rocky outcrops. Pass round the shoulder of **Rossköpfe** and bear R, ascending a little to contour across a mixture of rocky slopes and scree below Bitterichkopf. Pass the shoulder of Gebäudspitze R, and bear R to a path junction. Continue ahead and zigzag steeply up to **Gebäudjöchl** col (2452m) (**1hr 30min**).

Looking across the Medrioltal valley from the col, you will see a track coming up from Zams in the Inn valley. Württemberger Haus is visible ahead, perched on a bluff overlooking the valley. To get there, however, is not as straightforward as it looks. Turn L at the col, then bear back R across the scree slopes of Gebäudspitze to reach a path junction overlooking Auf der Lacke lake. Turn L, zigzag down the hillside and cross a small bridge over the Medriolbach to reach **Württemberger Haus** (2220m) (DAV, 56 beds 16b/40d, meals/refreshments, mid Jun–mid Sep, +43 676 397 5189, **www.wuerttemberger-haus.at**) (**30min**).

STAGE 21

Württemberger Haus to Memminger Hütte

Start	Württemberger Haus (2220m)
Finish	Memminger Hütte (2242m)
Distance	7km
Ascent	670m
Descent	650m
Grade	Black
Time	5hr
Highest point	Grossbergspitze (2657m)
Maps	ÖAV3/3 (1:25,000); FB5504 (1:35,000); K24 (1:50,000)
Access	No intermediate access

This challenging high-level stage requires mountain-trekking experience and a good head for heights. Ascending over tussock grass, scree and bare rock, with sections aided by fixed cables, the path climbs onto the Lechtaler Alpen ridge. Following the ridge over a series of crests, including Grossbergspitze, the path provides awesome views in all directions. This stage finishes with a final steep climb to Seescharte notch and a descent to Memminger Hütte.

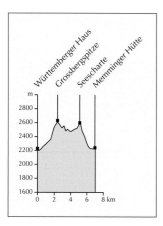

From **Württemberger Haus**, take a path heading WNW (sp Memminger Hütte) contouring across the slopes of Medriolkopf. Rounding a coomb, the path starts a long, steady ascent SW towards the gap between Spiessrutenspitze and Schieferspitze, which can be seen ahead. Initially across grassy slopes, the path becomes rockier after crossing a cleft.

Continue ascending across the screes below Südturm and bear R, zigzagging up rocky slopes with Schieferscharte notch R. There is one short section with fixed cables for security. Turn R and circle a small

Scrambling along the ridge between Grossbergspitze and Grossbergkopf

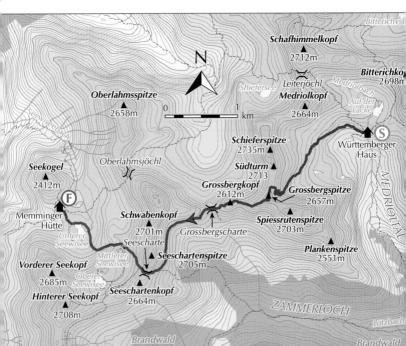

inclined plateau anticlockwise to reach the summit ridge. Scramble along this ridge to reach **Grossbergspitze** (2657m) (**2hr**).

From the summit, there are extensive views in all directions, with the east face of Parseierspitze dominating the view SW. Continue scrambling along the ridgeline, with some fixed cables, dropping down a little before rising to **Grossbergkopf** (2612m). Still following the ridge along an exposed crest, drop down to cross the head of **Grossbergscharte** notch (2493m). Shortly after the notch, drop down L, and contour across the rocky slopes and screes of Kleinberg. Down to the L is the deep Zammerloch valley and the path bears L, contouring around the bowl high above the valley head. Bear R beneath Seeschartenspitze R, then join a path coming up from Zams and ascend steeply to reach **Seescharte** notch (2599m) (**2hr**). The path to Zams is the route of the popular E5 trail from Bavaria to Northern Italy.

As you cross the ridge, the view down is a glaciated landscape of cirques and lakes sitting above the side of Parseiertal, with Memminger Hütte beyond. The path zigzags off the ridge before bearing R to descend across rocky slopes. Cross the stream just below the outlet from **Mittlerer Seewisee** lake to reach a path junction (2409m) (**15min**).

Turn R and follow the path down through a tiny ravine, then circle **Unterer Seewisee** lake L, to arrive at **Memminger Hütte** (2242m) (DAV, 132 beds 20b/112d, meals/refreshments, early Jun–late Sep, +43 676 746 0208, www.memmingerhuette.com) (**45min**). As Memminger Hütte is an overnight stop on the E5 trail, it can become very busy during peak periods. Try to arrive early!

Memminger Hütte stands above Unterer Seewisee lake

STAGE 22

Memminger Hütte to Ansbacher Hütte

Start	Memminger Hütte (2242m)
Finish	Ansbacher Hütte (2376m)
Distance	10km
Ascent	1040m
Descent	910m
Grade	Black
Time	6hr
Highest point	Griesslscharte (2632m)
Maps	ÖAV3/3 (1:25,000); FB5504 (1:35,000); K24 (1:50,000)
Access	No intermediate access

This is another challenging stage. A steep descent into Parseiertal valley is followed by an ascent up the screes of Langkar cirque (where snow may remain all year) and through a narrow chimney with fixed cables to Griesslscharte notch. The path then follows the main Lechtaler Alpen ridge, running just below the ridgeline, and crossing it two more times, before a short descent S to Ansbacher Hütte and a first distant view of St Anton.

Leave **Memminger Hütte** on a path N to reach a path junction after 150 metres. Turn L (sp Ansbacher Hütte) and start descending diagonally across the hillside SW. For the next 3km the path drops down into **Parseiertal**, initially on grassy slopes but passing through patches of forest below 1900m altitude. As the path descends, it crosses a number of side valleys. Just before you reach the valley floor a small metal bridge takes the path across a fissure in the hillside. At the bottom (1723m), cross the streambed by stepping stones, although the stream is often dry by midsummer (**1hr 20min**).

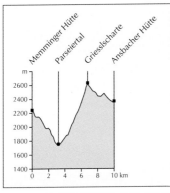

Turn R on the other bank, climbing diagonally away from the stream. Bear L round a shoulder of Griesslspitze and start the long ascent of **Langkar**. In the next 3.5km the path climbs continuously, gaining 900m in altitude. Initially contouring across grassy slopes to the L of the valley, the path soon crosses the stream and zigzags up **Schafgufel** to reach a path junction (1977m) (**50min**).

Bear L and continue ascending grassy slopes, now to the R of the

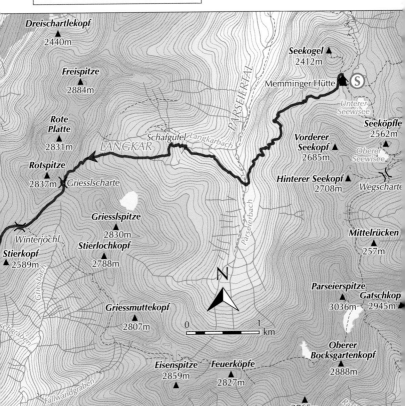

Griesslscharte notch and Rotspitze with its red rock clearly visible

valley. After 2100m altitude, the grass ends, the path continuing steeply up rocks and scree. From here to the col, patches of snow may remain all year. Towards the head of Langkar the gradient steepens and the path crosses to the L of the valley, where fixed cables aid the final ascent up a narrow chimney to **Griesslscharte** notch (2632m) (**2hr**).

The notch represents a crossing of the Lechtaler Alpen watershed, and between here and Ansbacher Hütte the path remains close to the ridgeline, crossing it two more times. Circle a small boulder-filled cirque clockwise, then bear R, descending gently across stony slopes where snow often lies all year. Views ahead are extensive with the Silvretta range, on the borders of Austria and Switzerland, visible on the horizon. The path drops down across the scree and rock of Oberes Griessl, then rises slightly to pass a path junction L and recross the ridge at **Winterjöchl** (2528m) (**40min**).

The path drops down a little on the north side of the col, then continues contouring across scree parallel to the ridge. The final crossing of the watershed involves a short steep scramble up **Kopfscharte** notch (2484m) (**40min**).

Continue ascending gently for a short distance on grassy slopes along the S side of the ridge, then descend SW across scree, bearing R below Stierköpfl to reach a path junction. The path R leads to Kaiserjochhaus, and is the route of the next stage. Turn L and contour across the grassy slopes of **Schafnock**. Pass a path junction L and ascend slightly to reach **Ansbacher Hütte** (2376m) (DAV, 65 beds 27b/38d, meals/refreshments, early Jun–late Sep, +43 676 842 927 136, **www. ansbacherhuette.at**) (**30min**).

STAGE 23
Ansbacher Hütte to Leutkircher Hütte

Start	Ansbacher Hütte (2376m)
Finish	Leutkircher Hütte (2251m)
Distance	12.5km
Ascent	970m
Descent	1080m
Grade	Black
Time	7hr
Highest point	Hinterseejoch (2482m)
Maps	ÖAV3/3 (1:25,000); FB5504 (1:35,000); K24 (1:50,000)
Access	No intermediate access

This is another challenging high-level route with stiff ascents, vertical drop-offs, scree and rock. The path rises and falls over two cols before following the Theodor-Haas-Weg across the SE face of rugged Vorderseespitze, with steep drop-offs protected by fixed cables. The route crosses two more cols as the path wanders from side to side across the Lechtaler Alpen ridge before descending across scree to Kaiserjochhaus. After a short but steep ascent to Schindlescharte, with some aided sections, the route goes downhill to Leutkircher Hütte.

This stage starts by contouring N from **Ansbacher Hütte** over grassy slopes, returning up the Schafnock ridge, which was descended at the end of Stage 22. After 600 metres fork L (sp Kaiserjochhaus), ascending gently across the scree below Stierköpfl, to cross the ridge at **Flarschjoch** (2464m) (**25min**).

Over the col, the path drops 50m, zigzagging down to cross a small, dried-up karst lake, then continues descending gently across the scree to a path junction. Fork L, continuing to descend across scree to a grassy col with a shelter and a series of path junctions at **Alperschonjoch** (2303m) (**35min**).

The route from here to Hinterseejoch uses the **Theodor-Haas-Weg**, a tricky path across the rocky SE face of Vorderseespitze. To avoid this, drop down from Alperschonjoch to about 1900m altitude and turn R to follow a path ascending past Vordersee lake L. Rejoin the main path about 250 metres beyond the lake.

Continue ahead W, descending a little over grassy slopes before rising to contour across the exposed face of the mountain, with steep drop-offs and fixed cables for security. Contour across the scree of Verborgene Pleis cirque, staying about 50m above Vordersee lake, then bear R, zigzagging steeply up to **Hinterseejoch** (2482m) (**2hr**).

Cross the col and zigzag down the other side towards the bowl of Kridlon cirque. Turn L at a path

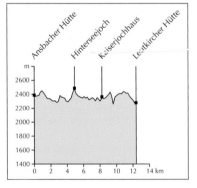

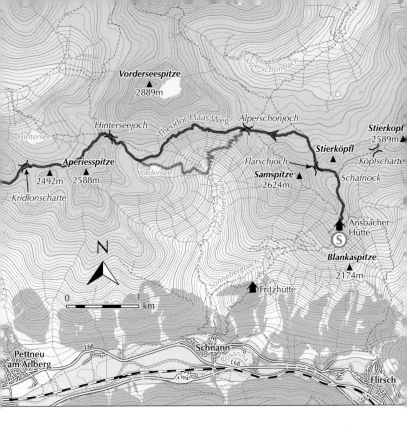

junction and continue descending before contouring across the screes below Furglerspitze, Aperiesspitze and Kridlonspitze, with Hintersee lake below R. The path ascends, aided by fixed cables and rungs, to **Kridlonscharte** notch (2371m), between Kridlonspitze and Kreuzkopf, where there is a view down into Stanzertal far below (**50min**).

Drop down from the notch SW, across grassy slopes and a boulder field, then scramble up a rocky hillside below Kreuzkopf and Griesskopf, aided by fixed cables, carefully following the red paint flashes as it is easy to go wrong. Zigzag up a grassy ridge and descend a little to reach **Kaiserjochhaus**, which can be seen on the col below (2310m) (DAV, 66 beds 19b/47d, meals/refreshments, end Jun–end Sep, +43 664 155 6533, **www.kaiserjochhaus.at**) (**1hr 10min**).

Leave Kaiserjochhaus on a path (sp Leutkircher Hütte) zigzagging W up a grassy ridge over **Kaiserkopf**, with a steep drop into a bowl R. Continue ascending

Leutkircher Hütte, with St Anton in the valley below

across grassy slopes towards **Schindlescharte** notch to a junction (**40min**) where a side path L leads to the summit of Schindlekopf.

Continue a short distance to the top of the col (2455m), then follow an undulating traverse below the screes of Stanskogel R. At **Gaisswasen** (**35min**) you reach a path junction R, where a side path leads up to Stanskogel summit.

Bear L, rounding the shoulder of Hirschpleiskopf, where views open out of St Anton and the extensively developed ski slopes on the mountainsides beyond Almajurjoch, and descend to a path junction R (**25min**). From here an eroded path drops down to **Leutkircher Hütte** (2251m) (DAV, 60 beds 15b/45d, meals/refreshments, late Jun–late Sep, +43 664 985 7849, **www.leutkircher-huette.at**) (**20min**). If you want to go straight to St Anton avoiding Ulmer Hütte, you can join Stage 21A at Leutkircher Hütte.

STAGE 24

Leutkircher Hütte to Arlbergpass

Start	Leutkircher Hütte (2251m)
Finish	Arlbergpass (1793m)
Distance	13.5km
Ascent	630m
Descent	1100m
Grade	Black
Time	5hr
Highest point	Valfagehrjoch (2539m)
Maps	ÖAV3/2 (1:25,000); FB5504 (1:35,000); K24 1:50,000)
Access	Cable cars from Kapall and Galzig to St Anton
	Bus from St Christoph to St Anton

The route starts by contouring the south-facing slopes of Bacherspitze and Weissschrofenspitze, including a steep descent aided by chains and rungs, to reach Ulmer Hütte, which sits below Pazüelfernerspitze. The final descent to the Arlbergpass summit follows a combination of 4WD tracks and good mountain paths through the Arlberg ski area, passing ski runs above St Anton and St Christoph. For most of this decent, St Christoph is visible in the valley far below.

From **Leutkircher Hütte**, follow a path SW (sp Ulmer Hütte), descending slightly across a rocky saddle to **Almajurjoch** (2237m) (**10min**) and continue ahead past a hunting lodge L. After 250 metres, fork L at a path junction and ascend steadily to another junction (**30min**) where a path L descends to Kapall and St Anton. Keep R ahead, climbing steeply on a zigzag path across the face of **Bacherspitze** to reach a high point (2477m) (**30min**).

Descend steeply for 750 metres on a path aided by chains and rungs to reach a low point (2342m) (**30min**), then start ascending steadily across the scree slopes below **Weissschrofenspitze** R. In places, winter washouts have created deep gullies in the scree, which need to be negotiated. Pass a path junction L (**25min**) and continue climbing across scree to reach a rock face. Scramble up, at first over glacially smoothed rocks then using steps cut into the rock, to reach **Matunjoch** (2519m) (**40min**).

Weissschrofenspitze (L) and Fallersteinspitze standing above the head of Almajurtal

Follow path ahead for 400 metres across a high saddle, where patches of snow can remain all year, to reach Valfagehrjoch col (2543m) (**10min**). Bear L and follow a good quality asphalt track winding downhill through a barren man-made landscape of ski tows, chairlifts and reservoirs for snow-making equipment to reach **Ulmer Hütte** (2285m) (DAV 46 beds 46b/0d, meals/refreshments, mid July–mid Sep, +43 5446 30200, www.ulmerhuette.at) (**20min**).

Leave the hut by a narrow zigzag path downhill from the SW corner of the building (sp Galzig) and turn L onto a gravel 4WD track heading SE through wide alpine pastures and follow this downhill.

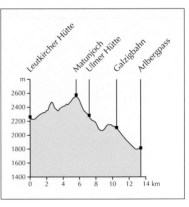

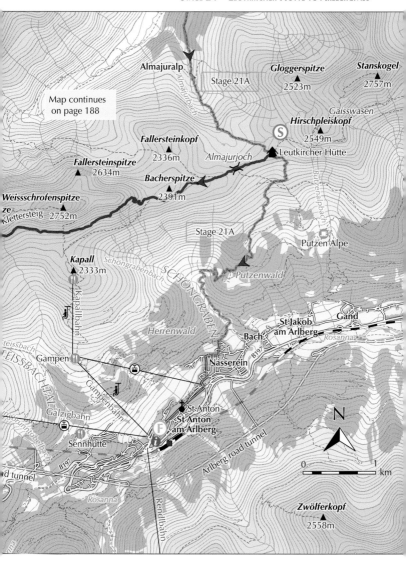

Almajuralp

Stage 21A

Gloggerspitze
▲ 2523m

Stanskogel
▲ 2757m

Gaisswasen

Map continues
on page 188

Hirschpleiskopf
▲ 2549m

Ⓢ

Fallersteinkopf
▲ 2336m

Almajurjoch

▲ Leutkircher Hütte

Fallersteinspitze
▲ 2634m

Bacherspitze
▲ 2391m

Weissschrofenspitze
ze
Klettersteig ▲ 2752m

Stage 21A

Putzen Alpe

Kapall
▲ 2333m

SCHÖNGRABEN

Putzenwald

Schöngrabenbach

St Jakob   Gand
am Arlberg
Bach   Rosanna

Herrenwald

Teissbach

Gampen

Nasserein

TEISSBACHTAL

St Anton
St Anton
am Arlberg

Galzigbahn

N

Sennhütte

Arlberg road tunnel

0   1
km

d tunnel

Rosanna

Zwölferkopf
▲ 2558m

187

Ignore a turn R to St Christoph and continue past a reservoir R to reach a junction of tracks at **Arlensattel** (2057m) (**20min**).

Turn R (sp Galzig Bergstation) on a narrow path that winds uphill, passing below the summit of **Galzig** L where there are three chairlift stations above the path. Continue under the St Christoph chairlift and follow the path, now winding downhill, past a TV transmission mast L to reach **Galzigbahn** cable-car station (2082m) (meals/refreshments) (**35min**).

Turn R on an asphalt road and follow this uphill past a depot for ski-run maintenance machinery then downhill round three hairpin bends. After the third bend, turn R onto a narrow path zigzagging down the hillside. Cross the asphalt road and follow the path downhill through Krummholz. Recross the road, turning R and L to continue downhill, then follow the path bearing R to reach **Maiensee** lake (1860m) (**25min**). At Maiensee the Adlerweg crosses Jakobsweg, part of the Camino pilgrim route from Austria to Santiago in Spain. A marker shows this as the highest point on the entire Camino.

Pass the lake L then cross the asphalt road for a third time, doglegging R and L to follow a faint track that uses boardwalks to wind across a boggy area. Where this ends, turn R at a T-junction then R again to pass behind an old wooden building that was formerly a restaurant on the edge of St Christoph. Fork R through a

An asphalt road descends steeply from Valfagehrjoch to Ulmer Hütte

Ulmer Hütte sits beneath the face of Pazielfernerspitze

gate onto a track then, where this turns R uphill, continue ahead on a narrow path winding past another marshy area R. Aim to pass about 50 metres to the R of a red/white electricity pylon, then follow the path bearing L to emerge on the main road at the *Passhöhe* (highest point) of the **Arlbergpass** beside an eagle sculpture and opposite the summit car park (1793m) (limited accommodation, meals/refreshments) (**25min**).

Congratulations, you have reached the end of the Adlerweg. Either celebrate in St Christoph or catch a bus to St Anton and celebrate in one of the many bars there. In summer there is a two-hourly bus service over the Arlbergpass, which takes 11min to reach St Anton am Arlberg from St Christoph. **St Anton am Arlberg** (1304m) (all services, accommodation, meals/refreshments, tourist office Dorfstrasse 8, +43 544 622690 **www.stantonamarlberg.com**, trains to Innsbruck, Vienna, Bregenz, Zurich). For a description of St Anton, see Stage 21A.

STAGE 19A

Boden to Häselgehr

Start	Boden (1356m)
Finish	Häselgehr church (1006m)
Distance	15.5km
Ascent	330m
Descent	680m
Grade	White
Time	4hr
Highest point	Boden, Hahntennjochstrasse (1392m)
Maps	ÖAV3/4 and 2/2 (1:25,000); FB351 (1:50,000); K24 (1:50,000)
Access	Bus to Boden from Elmen
	Bus from Häselgehr to Elmen, Reutte and Steeg

The route undulates gently as it descends on 4WD tracks and forest paths through the forests that line Hölltal and Bschlabertal, with views of Bschlabs across the valley. After emerging from the forest, the route crosses meadows to end at Häselgehr in the Lechtal valley.

Where Stage 19 reaches the beginning of **Boden**, turn R beside the fire station and bear L into the village. Turn R in front of the church and follow road N uphill past **Hinterleiten** hamlet to reach a junction with the Hahntennjoch pass road (1392m). Continue ahead, now descending gently and after 1km turn sharply L downhill on a gravel 4WD track (**30min**).

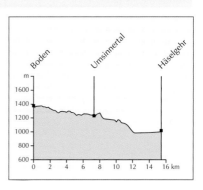

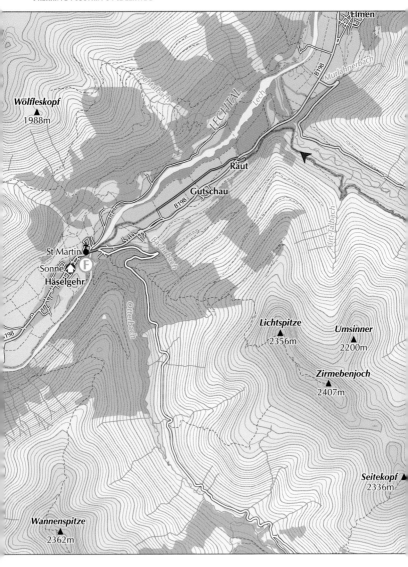

Mittlere Kreuzspitze
▲ 2496m

Bschlaber Kreuzspitze
▲ 2462m

Bortigscharte

Egger Muttekopf
▲ 2311m

Rotal

Sattel

Gstreinbach

BSCHLABERTAL

Brandkopf
▲ 1715m

Kanzertal

Mühlbach

Ortkopf
▲ 2314m

Kreuzjoch

Windegg   Egg
Bschlabs
Maria Schee ● Gemutlichkeit
                Zwiesle

EMSINNERTAL

Inerbach

Salvesenbach

HÖHERL

PLÖTZIGTAL

Plötzigbach

Ort der Stille ●

L266

Hinterleiten

Stage 19

Boden   Brandegg
Bergheimat ○ †
    St Joseph Ⓢ   Pfafflar

Hahntennbach

N

0   1
km

ANGERLETAL

Sattele

Gstreinbach

193

Follow track, turning sharply R at a hairpin bend. Track coming in L at the hairpin bend is the original route from Boden, which has been blocked permanently by a major washout. Bear L on a bridge over a spectacular river gorge (1297m) and turn immediately R, ascending into forest along the S side of **Hölltal** valley. A series of hairpins, passing a feeding station for deer, takes the track down into and across a deep-sided valley. The track continues contouring for 1.5km until it ends overlooking **Umsinnertal** (**1hr 20min**).

Bschlabs church seen from the opposite side of Bschlabertal

Continue on a narrow forest path climbing alongside Umsinnertal for 200 metres, then drop down to cross the river by a wooden bridge. It is 1km on faint forest paths to the start of another 4WD track. There are red paint markings on trees, but some have disappeared where there has been forest clearance. Climb steeply up the other side through woods to reach the ridgeline. Continue across two large clearings, where trees have been cut down, and along the crest of a small ridge before dropping down L to cross a stream and pick up the next 4WD track (**40min**).

Follow this for 3.5km, contouring along the S side of **Bschlabertal** and passing round two coombs. The track eventually descends to reach the main road in Lechtal (**45min**).

Turn L on a side road parallel to the main road then pass a road maintenance depot at **Raut** (992m) and immediately drop down R to pass under the road. Turn L onto an asphalt track heading through fields with occasional barns. Where this track turns sharply L, continue ahead to reach the banks of the river Lech and climb up to reach Häselgehr bridge. Turn R across the bridge to reach the stage end at **Häselgehr** church (1006m) (accommodation, meals/refreshments, shops, bus to Steeg) (**45min**).

STAGE 20A
Häselgehr to Steeg

Start	Häselgehr church (1006m)
Finish	Steeg bridge (1124m)
Distance	19.5km
Ascent	220m
Descent	100m
Grade	White
Time	4hr 30min
Highest point	Steeg (1124m)
Maps	ÖAV2/2 and 3/3 (1:25,000); FB5504 (1:35,000); K24 (1:50,000)
Access	Frequent bus service along Lechtal between Steeg and Reutte

This almost level walk along the pastoral Lechtal valley passes villages famous for the use of a distinctive form of wall painting known as *Lüftlmalerei*, which adorns many houses. The route is mostly along surfaced paths through fields, sometimes along the banks of the Lech.

The stage starts at **Häselgehr** church. Follow the main road SW for 150 metres and fork R before a barn onto a surfaced track. Cross a junction (sp Griessau) and continue above the houses parallel with the main road. You are now heading SW and will continue to head in this direction for 20km. Continue out of Häselgehr through

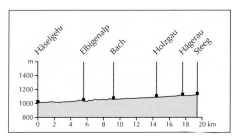

fields and a farmyard at Schönau. At **Ort**, turn R along the main road for 100 metres and then L (sp Elbigenalp) to reach the river. Turn R alongside the river to Griessau bridge (1021m) (**45min**).

Turn L over the bridge into **Griessau**, then

Faulewand-Spitze
2473m

Ilfenspitze
2535m

Wolfebnerspitze
2427m

Söllerkopf
2402m

ALLGÄUERALPEN

Hermannskarturm
2466m

Rotwan
2262m

Strahlkopf
2389m

Rothorn
2392m

Mutte
2187m

Geierwally
open-air
theatre

Untergiblen

Stienebach

Jöchelspitze
2226m

Lachenkopf
1945m

Modertalbach

B198

Untergrünau

Obergrünau

Obergiblen

Bühel

Lech

Bach

Unter
Winkel

Vaale Hölzgau

Schönau

Stockach

B198

Unter
Stockach

Sulzlbach

Brunnenkarunse

Alpersdobach

MADAUTAL

SULZTAL

Sulzlbach

Map continues
on page 198

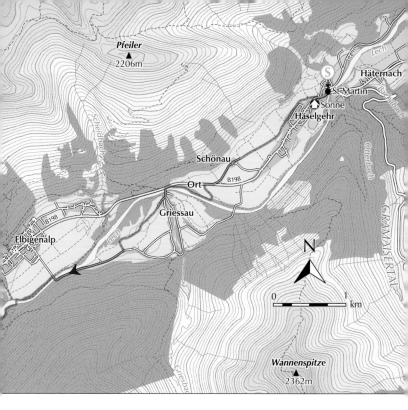

bear R and cross a stream. Continue out of the village for 1km on a path between fields, curving L to reach a minor road. Turn R and, with trees on your L, follow this road to reach the river. After 1km, cross the river on a modern bridge (one of a number of impressive bridges built since a devastating flood in 2005) and turn immediately L along the opposite bank (**30min**). To visit Elbigenalp continue ahead after crossing the bridge (all services, accommodation, meals/refreshments, tourist office Untergiblen 23, +43 563 45315, **www.lechtal.at**, bus service, wood-carving school and museum) (**10min**).

There are a variety of routes between **Elbigenalp** and **Steeg** following both banks of the river, and you may be faced with junctions where Steeg is sign-posted in both directions! Do not worry; so long as you head upstream, you will reach Steeg whichever path you choose.

Follow the river, crossing back to the south bank at the next new bridge (sp Grünau and Bach). Turn R to follow the river on a path winding through trees. After a little while, this path moves away from the river and continues with trees L and fields R, through the little hamlet of **Untergrünau**. Walk on through Obergrünau, bearing L to reach the river again and continue to **Bach** (1062m) (accommodation, meals/refreshments, supermarket, bus service) (**50min**).

Cross a bridge over the river Alperschonbach and turn L to follow the main road through the village. Just after a supermarket R, fork R on a path through fields. After 500 metres, turn L (sp Steeg cycle path) and after another 100 metres turn R. Continue for 1.5km, passing frequent barns and a small wayside chapel L, with Unter Stockach away L. When this path ends, turn L to reach the church at **Stockach** (**35min**).

Turn R and follow the main road through the village. Where the road bears R to cross the river, do not cross but continue ahead across a side stream (sp Holzgau) with the river R to reach after 500 metres a footbridge R. Cross the river and turn L, along the north bank, with Holzgau visible ahead, to reach a bridge over a side stream after 1.5km (**40min**).

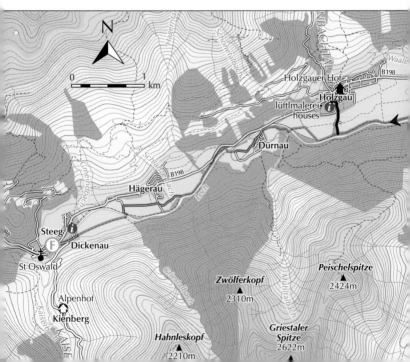

Following severe floods that swept away many bridges, several new footbridges have been built over the Lech

The path passes S of **Holzgau** (1114m) (all services, accommodation, meals/refreshments, tourist office Dorfplatz 45, +43 5633 5356). **Holzgauer Hof** (ÖAV associate, 35 beds 35b/0d, House 66, +43 5633 5250, www.holzgauerhof.at). To reach the village, famous for its Lüftlmalerei house decoration, turn R before the bridge and follow a path into the village (**10min**).

Continue along the riverside (sp Steeg) before turning away at a fork R. Soon after, turn L and cross to the south bank at the next bridge. Turn R, continuing to follow the river past a bridge and through **Dürnau** (1095m) (**20min**).

The path moves a little away from the river, past the Hammerle apartment complex L. About 500 metres after **Dürnau**, cross the river on another new bridge. Turn L along the N bank to follow the river for 800 metres and then continue on a path through fields. At an offset path junction, turn R and immediately L, passing S of **Hägerau** (1107m) (accommodation, meals/refreshments, supermarket, bus service) (**25min**).

At a T-junction turn L. Upon reaching the river, turn L, walking a short distance downstream to cross the river and then turn R on a path through fields lined with barns to Dickenau. Continue ahead to reach the end of the stage at **Steeg** bridge (1124m) (all services, accommodation, meals/refreshments, tourist office Aqua Nova +43 5633 5308, bus service) (**25min**). To continue directly onto Stage 21A, turn steeply uphill L after house 16, which is 100 metres before the bridge.

LÜFTLMALEREI: WHIMSICAL DECORATION IN LECHTAL

Lüftmalerei (air painting) is a common form of decoration in Lechtal, particularly in Holzgau

Many houses in the Lechtal valley are decorated in a style known as Lüftlmalerei, literally 'air painting'. This style, which originated in Southern Bavaria, is a rustic combination of *trompe l'oeil* and late baroque. The name comes from a house called 'Zum Lüftl' in Oberammergau, where Franz Zwink (1748–1792) pioneered the style. Images often have a religious theme, but not necessarily so, and are usually whimsical in character. Most are painted on the facade, where the colour lasts for about three generations, but others are found inside.

The trompe l'oeil element is usually portrayed in the depiction of architectural features, such as architraves, ledges and window surrounds, which in reality do not exist. The baroque is provided by whimsical characters somehow overlaid on the facade, such as people balanced on a ledge or floating on a cloud. Some of the best examples in Lechtal can be found in Holzgau; these include Dengeleshaus (Dorfplatz 49), Doppelhaus (Heimat museum 34/35), Adeg-Markt Hammerle (50), and Lippa-Franzhaus (32).

STAGE 21A

Steeg to St Anton am Arlberg

Start	Steeg bridge (1124m)
Finish	St Anton am Arlberg town hall (1284m)
Distance	19.5km (20km via Kaisers)
Ascent	1190m
Descent	1030m
Grade	Red
Time	7hr (7hr 30min via Kaisers)
Highest point	Leutkircher Hütte (2251m)
Maps	ÖAV3/2 (1:25,000); FB5504 (1:35,000); K24 (1:50,000)
Access	Bus from Steeg to Reutte, Lech and Kaisers. Train from St Anton to Innsbruck, Bregenz and Zurich

This stage follows forest paths and a surfaced road ascending from Steeg to Kaisers, then continues along a 4WD track and steeply up a path through forest and alpine meadows to Leutkircher Hütte. From here your final objective, St Anton am Arlberg, is visible in the valley below, and a straightforward descent on a mix of paths and forestry roads takes you 1000m down to the town.

From the main bridge in **Steeg** follow Dickenau E along the S side of the river. After house 15, turn R at a sharp bend and head steeply uphill on a surfaced road (sp Kaisers). After 150 metres, turn L on a footpath into the forest and follow this winding uphill steeply. Pass Steeg waterworks and continue on the forest path to rejoin the road. The gradient eases as the road contours along the side of the Kaisertal valley, high above the river Kaiserbach, to reach the tiny village of **Kienberg** (1297m) and **Gasthof Alpenhof** (private, accommodation, +43 676 703 9761, **www.alpenhof-lorenz.at**) (**40min**).

The road continues towards Kaisers, passing through avalanche shelters, and after 700 metres reaches a fork (**15min**). The direct route to Leutkircher Hütte takes the lower fork R, contouring above the river and passing 150m below Kaisers.

Map continues on page 204

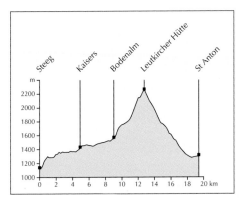

To visit Kaisers

The upper fork L continues climbing, and after 1.5km reaches **Kaisers**, a community of isolated farms and houses connected by the road as it zigzags up the hillside. Soon after the first farm R, there is a faint unsignposted field path L. This cuts off the zigzags and heads directly to the top of the village and **Edelweisshaus** (1530m).

If you miss the path, stay on the road around two hairpin bends to reach the refuge (DAV, 32 beds 23b/9d, meals/refreshments, mid May–end Oct, +43 5633 51158, **www.dav-edelweisshaus.at**) **(45min)**.

From the refuge follow the surfaced road back downhill, past the church R and round a hairpin bend. Take a faint field path L, descending through meadows to rejoin the direct route to Leutkircher Hütte in the valley below, where you turn L **(15min)**.

Main route

The direct track continues past chalets at Boden, and after being rejoined by the route through Kaisers, turns R to cross the river by a bridge (1384m) **(25min)**. Bear R uphill on a surfaced road, which becomes a 4WD track after a junction (sp Leutkircher Hütte). This track, which you follow for 4.5km, climbs gently SW along the side of **Almajurtal** valley. After 2km, drop down R to cross the river, crossing back after a further 2km. At the point where the 4WD track forks just before **Bodenalm** pasture hut (snacks/refreshments, start Jun–mid Sep), leave the track and turn L (sp Leutkircher Hütte) across a meadow to pick up a path that enters the forest just R of the stream (1554m) **(1hr 25min)**.

Zigzag steeply up through the trees, bearing R at the top and continue alongside a meadow at Moos. Just before the path crosses the stream to reach **Almajuralp** farm (1805m), turn L up through the trees **(1hr)**.

Continue ascending, on an eroded path through shrubs and dwarf conifers, onto a grassy hillside with rocky outcrops above, to reach **Leutkircher Hütte**, which sits on the ridge L of Almajurjoch col (2251m) (DAV, 60 beds 15b/45d, meals/ refreshments, late Jun–late Sep, +43 664 985 7849, **www.leutkircher-huette.at**)

(**1hr 20min**). At Leutkircher Hütte the path crosses Stage 24 of the main route through the Lechtal Alpen.

From Leutkircher Hütte a stony path (sp St Anton) descends SE then S and finally SW across grassy meadows. Pass a small chalet with a balcony L and continue straight ahead at a path junction. Reaching the treeline, pass through dwarf conifers and cross a 4WD track. Continue down through bigger trees. At an unmarked path junction, turn R, cutting through a small ridge to drop down to a good quality 4WD track just before a sharp hairpin bend (**50min**).

Turn R and follow the track as it zigzags down into Schöngraben valley. Some of the bends can be shortened by obvious cut-offs. Pass a 4WD track L and continue around a bend R to reach a bridge R, just before passing under power cables (**30min**).

Cross the bridge and fork L along the opposite bank on a track that soon becomes surfaced. Passing the end of the winter *Rodelbahn* (toboggan run), you reach the St Anton suburb of **Nasserein**. Continue on this road round a series of bends L and R, passing numerous apartments and ski chalets, to reach the base station of the Nasserein cablecar (**20min**).

Further on, the road reaches Dorfstrasse, the main street through St Anton. Turn R and follow this street for 1.1km to reach the town hall, L, in the centre of **St Anton** (1284m) (all facilities, accommodation, meals/refreshments, tourist office Dorfstrasse 8, +43 5446 22690 www.stantonamalberg.com, bus and railway stations) (**15min**).

St Anton town centre

ST ANTON AM ARLBERG, CRADLE OF ALPINE SKIING

For many centuries, St Anton was a quiet backwater in a remote corner of Tyrol. A narrow mule track over the Arlberg pass facilitated some trading to take place, mostly of salt. In 1824, the track was widened and surfaced, enabling the use of wheeled transport. Soon after, in the 1840s, the British surveyed the route as a possible rail link to Egypt, but this came to nothing. It was not until 1884 that the 10km Arlberg rail tunnel was opened, putting St Anton on a key east–west route through the Alps. (Arlberg is the watershed between rivers flowing to the North Sea and to the Black Sea.) The town became a stopping point for the 'Arlberg Orient Express', which provided a first-class-only wagons-lits service from Paris to Budapest, with a connection from London.

The arrival of the railway opened up the St Anton and Arlberg region to tourists. Originally, tourists were attracted by the delights of summer; however, the formation of the Ski Club in 1901 and the pioneering efforts of some of Europe's first ski instructors led to St Anton developing into a world-class winter sports resort. Today the Arlberg ski region, of which St Anton is the largest part, is the third most important skiing area in Tyrol, with a long season from late Nov to late Apr/early May. There are more than 300km of pistes and 200km of off-piste skiing, served by 88 lifts; it held the world skiing championships in 2001. The town has a wide variety of accommodation and many restaurants and bars, making it an ideal place to relax and celebrate the completion of your Adlerweg walk.

APPENDIX A
Distances, timings and facilities

Timings are based on an average walker carrying a moderate pack in good weather conditions and walking each stage without stopping. You can plan your own schedule but always remember to allow ample time to reach each night's accommodation. Entries in brackets are off-route.

Stage	Location	Distance (km)	Time (h:m)	Altitude (m)	Hotel/ guest house	Refuge/ unserviced	Meals	Pasture hut	Tourist office	Bus service	Railway station
Section 1 Kaisergebirge											
1	**St Johann station**			670	H				T	B	S
	Rummlerhof	4.0	0:50	780			M				
	Diebsöfen cave	2.9	1:20	1086			M				
	Schleierwasserfall	1.1	0.30	1158							
	(Ackerlhütte)	(1.7)	(0.45)	(1465)		(U)					
	Obere Regalm	2.3	1:00	1315							
	Baumgartenköpfl	1.1	0:35	1560				P			
	Gaudeamushütte	1.6	0:45	1263		R	M				
2	(Wochenbrunneralm)	(1.4)	(0.20)	(1085)			(M)			(B)	
	Gruttenhütte	1.6	1:30	1620		R	M				
	Wilder Kaiser Steig	2.9	0:45	1450							
	Kaiser Hochalm	2.7	1:00	1417							
	Steiner Hochalm	1.8	0:45	1257				P			

Stage	Location	Distance (km)	Time (h:m)	Altitude (m)	Hotel/ guest house	Refuge/ unserviced	Meals	Pasture hut	Tourist office	Bus service	Railway station
	Bärnstatt	1.7	0:45	918	H		M			B	
	Seestüberl	0.8	0:15	892	H		M			B	
	Schiesti	3.0	1:00	922	G		M			B	
3	Stöflalm/Walleralm	3.3	1:15	1148		R	M				
	Hochegg	1.6	1:00	1470							
	Steinbergalm	1.0	0:20	1293		R	M				
	Brentenjochalm	3.1	0:40	1204	G		M	P			
	(Aschenbrennerhaus)	(2.0)	(0:30)	(1135)	(H)		(M)				
	(Waldkapelle)	(3.3)	(0:45)	(698)							
	Kufstein	(1.3)	(0:30)	(499)	H		M		T	B	S
Section 2 Brandenberg Alpen and Rofangebirge											
4	Langkampfen station			489							S
	Unterlangkampfen	1.2	0:15	501	G		M			B	
	Höhlensteinhaus	3.0	1:50	1233			M				
	Köglhörndl	2.3	1:10	1645							
	Hundsalmjoch	2.4	1:25	1637							
	Buchackeralm	2.1	0:50	1324		R	M				
5	Nachberg Hochleger	4.8	2:05	1480							
	Plessenberg	2.8	1:40	1743							
	Kienberg	1.4	0:45	1786							
	Einkehralm	1.9	0:40	1446							

Stage	Location	Distance (km)	Time (h:m)	Altitude (m)	Hotel/ guest house	Refuge/ unserviced	Meals	Pasture hut	Tourist office	Bus service	Railway station
	Heubrandalm	1.5	0:20	1346							
	Pinegg	4.1	1:00	677	G		M			B	
6	Aschau	4.6	1:30	874			M			B	
	Haaser	1.0	0:15	911	G		M				
	Winm	1.8	0:35	1160							
	Lahnalm	2.2	0:45	1134							
	(Enterhof)	(2.0)	(0:40)	(1000)	(A)						
	Vordersteinberg	4.7	1:15	1043							
	Unterberg	1.7	0:30	1000	G		M			B	
(6A)	(Wimm)			(1160)							
	(Eilalm)	(2.3)	(0:55)	(1391)							
	(Labeggalm)	(1.7)	(0:40)	(1525)				(P)			
	(Kreuzeinalm Hochleger)	(1.5)	(0:35)	(1652)							
	(Zireinersee)	(2.6)	(1:20)	(1810)							
7	Durrahof	3.8	1:00	1014	A						
	Külermahdalm	2.3	0:40	1139							
	Schauertalalm	4.0	1:25	1250							
	Zireinersee	1.7	1:15	1810							
	Marchgatterl	1.1	0:35	1905							

Stage	Location	Distance (km)	Time (h:m)	Altitude (m)	Hotel/guest house	Refuge/unserviced	Meals	Pasture hut	Tourist office	Bus service	Railway station
	Rofan	1.2	0:45	2190							
	Grubascharte	1.2	0:25	2102							
	Mauritzalm	2.7	0:55	1834	G	R	M				
(7A)	(Marchgatterl)	(1905)									
	(Bayreuther Hütte)	(2.9)	(1:10)	(1576)		(R)	(M)	(P)			
	(Sonnwendbühlalm)	(1.9)	(0:40)	(1645)				(P)			
	(Schermsteinalm)	(3.2)	(1:20)	(1855)							
	(Krahnsattel)	(1.4)	(0:40)	(2002)							
	Mauritzalm	2.1	0:45	1834	G	R	M				
Section 3 Karwendelgebirge											
8	(Buchaueralm)		(0:50)	(1385)			(M)				
	Maurach	4.9	0:50	980	H		M		T	B	S
	Pertisau	4.3	1:05	952	H		M		T	B	
	Falzturnalm	3.6	0:55	1089			M			B	
	Gramaialm		1:00	1265	H		M	P		B	
	Lamsenjochhütte	4.2	2:00	1953		R	M				
9	Binsalm Niederleger	4.3	1:15	1500		R	M				
	(Alpengasthof Eng)	(1.9)	(1:30)	(1203)	(H)		(M)			(B)	
	Engalm	2.2	0:50	1237	G		(M)				
	Hohljoch	3.1	1:15	1794							
	Falkenhütte	2.9	1:10	1848		R	M				

Stage	Location	Distance (km)	Time (h:m)	Altitude (m)	Hotel/ guest house	Refuge/ unserviced	Meals	Pasture hut	Tourist office	Bus service	Railway station
10	von Barth monument	4.8	1:50	1399							
	Grasslegerbichl	2.5	1:10	1749							
	Karwendelhaus	1.7	0:30	1765		R	M				
11	Schlauchkarsattel	3.0	2:40	2639							
	Hinterautal	5.3	3:15	1205							
	Kastenalm	0.6	0:10	1220				P			
	Hallerangeralm	5.1	1:55	1768		R	M				
(11A)	(Angeralm)	(4.5)	(1:10)	(1310)							
	(Scharnitz turn-off)	(10.7)	(2:40)	(1050)							
	(Schönwies)	(1.1)	(0:25)	(980)	(H)						
	(Kastenalm)	(11.1)	(2:50)	(1220)				(P)			
	(Hallerangeralm)	(5.1)	(1:55)	(1768)		(R)	(M)				
12	Lafatscherjoch	2.1	1:00	(2081)							
	Stempeljoch	3.4	2:00	(2215)							
	Pfeishütte	1.9	0:30	(1922)		R	M				
	Mannlscharte	2.4	0:50	(2274)							
	Hafelekarhaus	3.2	1:10	(2269)			M				
Section 4 Innsbruck and Patscherkofel											
12A	**Innsbruck**			569	H		M		T	B	
	Bergisel	2.5	0:40	590			M			B	S

Stage	Location	Distance (km)	Time (h:m)	Altitude (m)	Hotel/ guest house	Refuge/ unserviced	Meals	Pasture hut	Tourist office	Bus service	Railway station
	Igls			870	H				T	B	
13	**Patscherkofel**			1964		R	M				
	Boscheben	2.3	0:45	2030		R	M				
	Tulfeinalm	5.7	1:45	2035			M				
	Halsmarter			1567			M				
	Tulfes			923	G				T	B	
	Hall in Tirol			565	H		M		T	B	S
Section 5 Wettersteingebirge and Mieminger Gebirge											
14	**Hochzirl station**			922							S
	Oberbach	3.8	1:40	1400							
	Solsteinhaus	3.2	1:20	1805		R	M				
15	Eppzirlerscharte	1.7	1:20	2102							
	Eppzirleralm	2.5	1:00	1459			M				
	Giessenbach	6.2	1:30	1000	G		M			B	S
	Hoher Sattel	3.3	1:35	1495							
	Weidach	4.3	1:05	1112	H		M		T	B	
16	Klamm	3.8	0:55	1170	G		M				
	(Hämmermoosalm)	(4.5)	(1:15)	(1417)		(R)	(M)				
	Gaistalalm	6.5	1:50	1366			M				
	Tillfussalm	0.8	0:15	1382		R	M				

Stage	Location	Distance (km)	Time (h:m)	Altitude (m)	Hotel/ guest house	Refuge/ unserviced	Meals	Pasture hut	Tourist office	Bus service	Railway station
	Igelsee	5.3	1:30	1543							
	Ehrwalder Alm	2.6	0:50	1502			M				
	Ganghofer Hütte	1.2	0:20	1289				P			
	Ehrwald	3.5	0:50	994	H				T		S
17	Lermoos	3.5	0:45	995	H				T	B	S
	Grubigstein	3.0	0:40	2028	G		M				
	Grubigalm			1712							
	Fernpass	4.5	1:25	1216	G		M			B	
	Schloss Fernstein	3.6	0:55	980	H	R	M			B	
	Loreahütte	4.4	2:45	2022		U					
Section 6 Lechtaler Alpen											
18	Tegestal	5.7	2:35	1392							
	Hintere Tarrentonalm	4.3	1:00	1519							
	Hinterbergjöchle	4.0	2:00	2203				P			
	Kromsattel	1.0	0:35	2137							
	Anhalter Hütte	1.0	0:20	2042		R	M				
19	Hahntennjoch	2.0	0:55	1894						B	
	Pfafflar	3.6	0:50	1619						B	
	Boden	1.7	0:30	1356	G		M			B	
	Hanauer Hütte	5.2	2:00	1922		R	M				

Stage	Location	Distance (km)	Time (h:m)	Altitude (m)	Hotel/ guest house	Refuge/ unserviced	Meals	Pasture hut	Tourist office	Bus service	Railway station
20	Hintere Dremelscharte	2.4	2:00	2470							
	Steinseehütte	1.9	1:15	2061		R	M				
	Rosskarscharte	3.0	1:45	2458							
	Gebäudjöchl	2.6	1:30	2452							
	Württemberger Haus	1.1	0:30	2220		R	M				
21	Grossbergerspitze	2.4	2:00	2657							
	Seescharte	2.7	2:00	2599							
	Memminger Hütte	1.9	1:00	2242		R	M				
22	Parseiertal	3.2	1:20	1723							
	Schafgufel	1.5	0:50	1977							
	Griesslscharte	2.0	2:00	2632							
	Winterjöchl	1.0	0:40	2528							
	Kopfscharte	1.1	0:40	2484							
	Ansbacher Hütte	1.2	0:30	2376		R	M				
23	Flarschjoch	1.0	0:25	2464							
	Alperschonjoch	1.5	0:35	2303							
	Hinterseejoch	2.4	2:00	2482							
	Kridlonscharte	1.3	0:50	2371							
	Kaiserjochhaus	1.9	1:10	2310		R	M				
	Schindlescharte	1.1	0:40	2455							

Stage	Location	Distance (km)	Time (h:m)	Altitude (m)	Hotel/ guest house	Refuge/ unserviced	Meals	Pasture hut	Tourist office	Bus service	Railway station
	Leutkircher Hütte	3.3	1:20	2251		R	M				
24	Matunjoch	5.6	2:45	2519			M				
	Ulmer Hütte	1.6	0:30	2285		R	M				
	Galzigbahn cable car	3.3	0:55	2082			M				
	Arlbergpass	3.0	0:50	1793	H		M			B	
Section 6A Lechtal valley											
(19A)	**(Boden)**			1356	(G)		(M)			(B)	
	(Umsinnertal)	(7.3)	(1:50)	1250							
	(Häselgehr)	(8.2)	(2:10)	1006	(G)		(M)			(B)	
(20A)	(Elbigenalp)	(5.6)	(1:15)	1040	(H)		(M)		(T)	(B)	
	(Bach)	(3.7)	(0:50)	1062	(H)		(M)				
	(Holzgau)	(5.2)	(1:15)	1114	(H)	(R)	(M)		(T)	(B)	
	(Hägerau)	(3.2)	(0:45)	1107	(H)		(M)				
	(Steeg)	(1.8)	(0:25)	1124	(H)		(M)		(T)	(B)	
(21A)	(Kienberg)	(1.6)	(0:40)	1297		(R)				(B)	
	(Kaisers)	(2.3)	(0:40)	1530			(M)			(B)	
	(Bodenalm)	(5.1)	(1:25)	1554				(P)			
	(Leutkircher Hütte)	(3.8)	(2:20)	2251		(R)	(M)				
	(Nasserein)	(5.8)	(1:40)	1290	(G)					(B)	
	(St Anton)	(0.9)	(0:15)	1284	(H)		(M)		(T)	(B)	(S)

APPENDIX B
Tourist offices

Stage 1
St Johann in Tirol
Poststrasse 2, St Johann 6380
+43 535 263 3350
www.kitzalps.cc

Going
Dorfstrasse 10, Going 6353
+43 505 09510
www.wilderkaiser.info/going

Ellmau
Dorf 35, Ellmau 6352
+43 505 09410
www.wilderkaiser.info/ellmau

Stage 2
Scheffau am Wilden Kaiser
Dorf 28
Scheffau am Wilden Kaiser 6306
+43 505 09310
www.wilderkaiser.info/scheffau

Stage 3
Kufstein
Unterer Stadtplatz 11–13
Kufstein 6330
+43 537 262 207
www.kufstein.com

Stage 4
Wörgl
Innsbrucker Strasse 1, Wörgl 6300
+43 575 077 000
www.kitzbueheler-alpen.com

Stages 5 and 7
Kramsach
Zentrum 1, Kramsach 6233
+43 533 721 200
www.alpbachtal.at

Stage 6
Achenkirch (for Steinberg)
Untere Dorfstrasse 387
Achenkirch 6215
+43 595 30050
www.achensee.com/tirol/steinberg

Stage 8
Maurach
Achenseestrasse 63
Maurach, 6212
+43 595 3000
www.achensee.com/tirol/maurach

Pertisau
Karwendelstrasse 10
Pertisau 6213
+43 595 30060
www.achensee.com/tirol/pertisau

Stage 9
Schwaz
Münchener Strasse 11
Schwaz 6130
+43 524 263 240
www.silberregion-karwendel.com

Stages 11 and 15
Scharnitz
Hinterautalstrasse 555b
Scharnitz 6108
+43 508 80540
www.seefeld.com/scharnitz

Stage 12
Innsbruck
Burggraben 3, Innsbruck 6020
+43 512 5356
www.innsbruck.info

Stage 13
Igls
Hilberstasse 15, Igls 6080
+43 512 5356 6080
www.innsbruck.info

Tulfes
Schmalzgasse 27, Tulfes 6075
+43 522 378 324
www.hall-wattens.at

Hall in Tirol
Unterer Stadtplatz 19
Hall in Tirol 6060
+43 522 345 544
www.hall-wattens.at

Stage 14
Zirl
Dorfplatz 2, Zirl 6170
+43 512 5356 6170
www.innsbruck.info

Stage 15
Seefeld
Bahnhofplatz 115, Seefeld 6100
+43 508 80
www.seefeld.com

Leutasch
Kirchplatzl 128a, Leutasch 6105
+43 508 80510
www.seefeld.com/leutasch-tirol

Stage 16
Ehrwald
Kirchplatz 1, Ehrwald 6632
+43 567 320 000 200
www.zugspitzarena.com

Stage 17
Lermoos
Unterdorf 15, Lermoos 6631
+43 567 320 000 300
www.zugspitzarena.com

Nassereith
Postplatz 28, Nassereith 6465
+43 541 269 1041
www.imst.at

Stage 19
Imst
Johannesplatz 4, Imst 6460
+43 541 26910
www.imst.at

Stage 20
Landeck
Malserstrasse 10, Landeck 6500
+43 544 265 600
www.tirolwest.at

Stages 24 and 21A
St Anton
Dorfstrasse 8, St Anton 6580
+43 544 622 690
www.stantonamarlberg.com

Stage 20A
Elbigenalp
Untergiblen 23, Elbigenalp, 6652
+43 563 45315
www.lechtal.at

Holzgau
Dorfplatz 45, Holzgau 6654
+43 563 35356
www.lechtal.at

Steeg
Aqua Nova, Steeg 6655
+43 563 35308
www.lechtal.at

APPENDIX C
Useful contacts

Organisations
Austrian Alpine Club (UK)
Unit 43, Glenmore Business Park
Blackhill Road, Holton Heath
Poole BH16 6NL
+44 192 955 6870
aac.office@aacuk.org.uk
www.alpenverein.at/britannia

Österreichischer Alpenverein
Olympiastrasse 37
Innsbruck 6020, Austria
+43 512 59547-0
office@alpenverein.at
www.alpenverein.at

Tirol Werbung (tourism promotion board)
Maria-Theresien-Strasse 55
Innsbruck 6020, Austria
+43 512 7272-0
www.tirol.at
www.tirol.at/reisefuehrer/sport/wandern/
adlerweg

Maps and guides
Stanfords
7 Mercer Walk
Covent Garden
London WC2H 9FA
0207 836 1321
sales@stanfords.co.uk
www.stanfords.co.uk

The Map Shop
15 High St
Upton upon Severn
Worcester WR8 0HJ
0800 085 40 80
or 01684 593146
themapshop@btinternet.com
www.themapshop.co.uk

Freytag & Berndt
www.freytagberndt.com

Kompass Karten
www.kompass.de

SummitLynx (digital tracking app)
www.summitlynx.com

Travel
ÖBB (Austrian Railways)
+43 51717
www.oebb.at

Deutsche Bahn (German Railways)
+49 302970 (German)
+49 30311682904 (English)
www.bahn.com

RailEurope (international rail tickets)
www.raileurope.com

Trainline (international rail tickets)
www.thetrainline.com

Safety
Bergwetter Österreich
(mountain weather forecast)
www.wetter.orf.at/tirol/bergwetter

Bergrettungsdienst (mountain rescue)
Tel 112 (emergency services number)

APPENDIX D

Glossary of German geographic terms

German	English	German	English
Ache	river	*Haupt*	main/chief
Alm	mountain pasture	*Haus*	house/inn
alt	old	*hinter*	behind/after
Aussichtspunkt	viewpoint	*hoch*	high
Autobahn	motorway	*höhen*	height
Bach	stream/brook	*Höhenlinien*	contour lines
(Eisen)Bahn	railway	*Höhenpunkt*	highpoint
Bahnhof	railway station	*Höhle*	cave
Bauernhof	farm	*Hütte*	hut/cottage/refuge
Berg	hill/mountain	*Jagdhütte*	hunting lodge
Boden	land/bottom/floor	*Joch*	col
Brück	bridge	*Karrenweg*	bridleway
Denkmal	monument	*Kette*	(mountain) range
Dorf	village	*Klamm*	gorge
Fahrweg	dirt road	*Klettersteig*	aided climbing trail
Festung	fortress	*Kirche*	church
Friedhof	cemetery	*Kopf*	head/hilltop
Fussweg	footpath	*(Weg)Kreuz*	(wayside) cross
Gasse	lane/alley	*Land*	region/state
Gebirge	mountain range	*Langlauf*	cross country ski
Gemeinde	local district	*Mautstrasse*	toll road
Gipfel	summit	*Mauer*	wall
Gletscher	glacier	*neu*	new
Grenze	boundary		

German	English	German	English
nieder	low/lower	*Sessellift*	chairlift
obere	upper	*Spitze*	peak
Passhöhe	summit	*Stadt*	town
Pfarr	parish	*Steig*	trail
Piste	ski run	*Steinbruch*	quarry
Quelle	spring	*Strasse*	street
rot	red	*Tal*	valley
Sattel	saddle/ridge	*vordere*	front/near
Schloss	castle	*Wald*	wood/forest
schwarz	black	*Waldgrenze*	treeline
See	lake	*Wasserfall*	waterfall
Seilbahn	cable car	*Weg*	way
Sender	communications mast	*weiss*	white

STAMPS

STAMPS

STAMPS

STAMPS

STAMPS

STAMPS

DOWNLOAD THE ROUTES
IN GPX FORMAT

All the routes in this guide are available for download from:

www.cicerone.co.uk/1090/GPX

as standard format GPX files. You should be able to load them into most online GPX systems and mobile devices, whether GPS or smartphone. You may need to convert the file into your preferred format using a conversion programme such as gpsvisualizer.com or one of the many other such websites and programmes.

When you follow this link, you will be asked for your email address and where you purchased the guidebook, and have the option to subscribe to the Cicerone e-newsletter.

www.cicerone.co.uk

LISTING OF CICERONE GUIDES

BRITISH ISLES CHALLENGES, COLLECTIONS AND ACTIVITIES

Cycling Land's End to John o' Groats
Great Walks on the England Coast Path
The Big Rounds
The Book of the Bivvy
The Book of the Bothy
The Mountains of England & Wales:
  Vol 1 Wales
  Vol 2 England
The National Trails
Walking the End to End Trail

SHORT WALKS SERIES

Short Walks Hadrian's Wall
Short Walks in Arnside and Silverdale
Short Walks in Nidderdale
Short Walks in the Lake District: Windermere Ambleside and Grasmere
Short Walks in the Surrey Hills
Short Walks on the Malvern Hills

SCOTLAND

Ben Nevis and Glen Coe
Cycle Touring in Northern Scotland
Cycling in the Hebrides
Great Mountain Days in Scotland
Mountain Biking in Southern and Central Scotland
Mountain Biking in West and North West Scotland
Not the West Highland Way
Scotland
Scotland's Mountain Ridges
Scottish Wild Country Backpacking
Skye's Cuillin Ridge Traverse
The Borders Abbeys Way
The Great Glen Way
The Great Glen Way Map Booklet
The Hebridean Way
The Hebrides
The Isle of Mull
The Isle of Skye
The Skye Trail
The Southern Upland Way
The Speyside Way Map Booklet
The West Highland Way
The West Highland Way Map Booklet
Walking Ben Lawers, Rannoch and Atholl
Walking in the Cairngorms
Walking in the Pentland Hills
Walking in the Scottish Borders
Walking in the Southern Uplands
Walking in Torridon, Fisherfield, Fannichs and An Teallach

Walking Loch Lomond and the Trossachs
Walking on Arran
Walking on Harris and Lewis
Walking on Jura, Islay and Colonsay
Walking on Rum and the Small Isles
Walking on the Orkney and Shetland Isles
Walking on Uist and Barra
Walking the Cape Wrath Trail
Walking the Corbetts:
  Vol 1 South of the Great Glen
  Vol 2 North of the Great Glen
Walking the Galloway Hills
Walking the John o' Groats Trail
Walking the Munros
  Vol 1 – Southern, Central and Western Highlands
  Vol 2 – Northern Highlands and the Cairngorms
Winter Climbs: Ben Nevis and Glen Coe

NORTHERN ENGLAND ROUTES

Cycling the Reivers Route
Cycling the Way of the Roses
Hadrian's Cycleway
Hadrian's Wall Path
Hadrian's Wall Path Map Booklet
The C2C Cycle Route
The Coast to Coast Cycle Route
The Coast to Coast Walk
The Coast to Coast Walk Map Booklet
The Pennine Way
The Pennine Way Map Booklet
Walking the Dales Way
Walking the Dales Way Map Booklet

NORTH-EAST ENGLAND, YORKSHIRE DALES AND PENNINES

Cycling in the Yorkshire Dales
Great Mountain Days in the Pennines
Mountain Biking in the Yorkshire Dales
St Oswald's Way and St Cuthbert's Way
The Cleveland Way and the Yorkshire Wolds Way
The Cleveland Way Map Booklet
The North York Moors
The Reivers Way
Trail and Fell Running in the Yorkshire Dales
Walking in County Durham
Walking in Northumberland
Walking in the North Pennines

Walking in the Yorkshire Dales: North and East
Walking in the Yorkshire Dales: South and West

NORTH-WEST ENGLAND AND THE ISLE OF MAN

Cycling the Pennine Bridleway
Isle of Man Coastal Path
The Lancashire Cycleway
The Lune Valley and Howgills
Walking in Cumbria's Eden Valley
Walking in Lancashire
Walking in the Forest of Bowland and Pendle
Walking on the Isle of Man
Walking on the West Pennine Moors
Walks in Silverdale and Arnside

LAKE DISTRICT

Bikepacking in the Lake District
Cycling in the Lake District
Great Mountain Days in the Lake District
Joss Naylor's Lakes, Meres and Waters of the Lake District
Lake District Winter Climbs
Lake District: High Level and Fell Walks
Lake District: Low Level and Lake Walks
Mountain Biking in the Lake District
Outdoor Adventures with Children – Lake District
Scrambles in the Lake District – North
Scrambles in the Lake District – South
Trail and Fell Running in the Lake District
Walking The Cumbria Way
Walking the Lake District Fells –
  Borrowdale
  Buttermere
  Coniston
  Keswick
  Langdale
  Mardale and the Far East
  Patterdale
  Wasdale
Walking the Tour of the Lake District

DERBYSHIRE, PEAK DISTRICT AND MIDLANDS

Cycling in the Peak District
Dark Peak Walks
Scrambles in the Dark Peak
Walking in Derbyshire
Walking in the Peak District – White Peak East
Walking in the Peak District – White Peak West

For full information on all our guides,
books and eBooks,
visit our website:
www.cicerone.co.uk